OCCASIONAL PAPER 86

Ghana: Adjustment and Growth, 1983–91

Ishan Kapur, Michael T. Hadjimichael,
Paul Hilbers, Jerald Schiff, and Philippe Szymczak

INTERNATIONAL MONETARY FUND
Washington DC
September 1991

Library of Congress Cataloging-in-Publication Data

Ghana—adjustment and growth, 1983–91 / by Ishan Kapur ...
[et al.].
    p. cm. — (Occasional paper (International Monetary Fund);
no. 86)
    "September 1991."
    Includes bibliographical references.
    ISBN 1-55775-182-X
    1. Structural adjustment (Economic policy) — Ghana. I. Kapur,
Ishan. II. Series.
HC1060.G425 1991   76469
338.9667'009'048 — dc20

                      TOC

                                        91-31829
                                        CIP

Price: US$10.00
(US$7.50 to full-time faculty members and
students at universities and colleges)

Please send orders to:
International Monetary Fund, Publication Services
700 19th Street, N.W., Washington, D.C. 20431, U.S.A.
Tel.: (202) 623-7430   Telefax: (202) 623-7201

Contents

Page

Box

Appendix

Charts

Section

Appendix

The following symbols have been used throughout this paper:

... to indicate that data are not available;

— to indicate that the figure is zero or less than half the final digit shown, or that the item does not exist;

– between years or months (e.g., 1990–91 or January–June) to indicate the years or months covered, including the beginning and ending years or months;

/ between years (e.g., 1990/91) to indicate a crop or fiscal (financial) year.

"Billion" means a thousand million.

Minor discrepancies between constituent figures and totals are due to rounding.

The term "country," as used in this paper, does not in all cases refer to a territorial entity that is a state as understood by international law and practice; the term also covers some territorial entities that are not states, but for which statistical data are maintained and provided internationally on a separate and independent basis.

Preface

This paper is based on internal staff reports and research papers prepared in connection with consultations between the IMF and Ghana during 1989–91 and includes information available through June 1991. The authors would like to acknowledge the support of officials of Ghana in the preparation of the paper. They are also indebted to Evangelos A. Calamitsis and Reinold H. van Til for their valuable comments, Ian McDonald and David Driscoll for editorial advice, and Elisabeth Baker for secretarial assistance. The authors bear sole responsibility for any factual errors.

The opinions expressed in the paper are those of the authors and should not be construed as representing the views of the Government of Ghana, Executive Directors of the IMF, or other members of the IMF staff.

I Introduction

Over the past eight years, Ghana has pursued a comprehensive program of financial and structural reforms, which has come to be perceived as an example of adjustment with growth. It was among the first sub-Saharan African countries to embark on such a reform program, and its efforts have been supported not only by successive arrangements with the IMF but also by bilateral and multilateral external financial assistance. As a consequence, Ghana's economic and financial performance has improved substantially after a prolonged period of economic decline, even though a number of structural and institutional constraints continue to confront the economy.

This paper highlights Ghana's reform efforts since 1983 and analyzes its experience with adjustment in four policy areas. Section II provides an overview of the economic strategy and economic and financial performance since 1983. Section III reviews the growth performance and developments in savings and investment balances, assessing the contribution by the public and private sectors in this regard.

Section IV presents the various stages of exchange reform and Ghana's exchange rate policy in general, reviews the outcome of these policies, and draws some policy lessons from Ghana's experience. The liberalization of the exchange and trade system has been a notable feature of the adjustment process in Ghana. It initially involved sizable discrete devaluations of the national currency, the cedi, followed by the introduction of a foreign exchange auction in September 1986, the legalization of the parallel exchange market in April 1988, and the eventual unification of the exchange markets in April 1990 in the context of an interbank system. These reforms were accompanied by the elimination of import licensing, reductions in import tariffs, and the lifting of virtually all restrictions on payments and transfers for current international transactions.

Section V surveys Ghana's fiscal adjustment, analyzing changes in government revenue and expenditure and their components, and emphasizing the distributional implications of the government's tax and expenditure policies. Fiscal adjustment since 1983 has resulted in a major reduction in fiscal imbalances and a strengthening of government savings, an expansion in tax receipts as a ratio to GDP, combined with far-reaching tax reforms to strengthen economic incentives and promote equity, and an expansion in social welfare spending and capital expenditure for the rehabilitation of economic infrastructure.

Section VI reviews monetary developments and policies since 1983. Special attention is given to the monetary authorities' gradual shift toward more market-oriented forms of monetary control. The main aim of monetary policy in Ghana over the past eight years has been to reduce the persistently high and sharply fluctuating rate of inflation. Inflation performance since 1983 is reviewed and the main determinants of changes in consumer prices are analyzed. It appears that, apart from monetary factors, inflation over the past years has been influenced by the domestic supply of food, and domestic (retail prices for petroleum products) and external (import prices) cost-push factors.

Finally, Section VII provides some concluding remarks on the main lessons to be drawn from Ghana's experience with adjustment, particularly with regard to the complementarity and sequencing of reforms.

II   Recent Economic Performance

ollowing a protracted period of economic decline, Ghana's economic and financial performance has improved substantially since the adoption by the Ghanaian authorities of an economic recovery program in April 1983. In the context of this program, the Government has implemented far-reaching financial and structural reforms, switching away from direct intervention and controls toward increased reliance on market-based instruments of policy.

Prior to 1983, inappropriate domestic policies and external shocks (droughts in 1975–77 and 1981–83 and a marked decline in the terms of trade) led to a severe worsening in economic and financial performance.[1] Large fiscal deficits, financed primarily by borrowing from the domestic banking system, gave rise to high rates of inflation and an increasingly overvalued exchange rate. Heavy government intervention in the economy through price, distribution, and import controls, as well as a massive expansion of the public sector through the establishment of a large number of state enterprises, exacerbated distortions in the economy and severely eroded incentives to produce, save, and invest. Export earnings fell sharply, while external financing, particularly from bilateral sources, virtually dried up, as creditors' confidence in the economy weakened. Shortages of foreign exchange and imported goods and distortions in the structure of relative prices led to a proliferation of parallel markets, an intensification of unrecorded cross-border trade, and a marked deterioration in government services, in the basic economic and social infrastructure, and in the country's capital stock in general. As a consequence, the growth of output had come to a halt and then turned negative, while real per capita income declined by more than 30 percent, inducing a large part of Ghana's relatively well-educated labor force to emigrate. The overall balance of payments deficit widened, giving rise to a depletion of gross official reserves and an accu-

mulation of external payments arrears of about US$580 million by the end of 1982.

Economic Strategy

Since 1983, Ghana's economic and financial strategy has been reoriented to lay the foundations for sustained output growth and the achievement of external payments viability over the medium term. The key elements of the strategy have been (a) a realignment of relative prices to encourage productive activities and exports and a strengthening of economic incentives; (b) a progressive shift away from direct controls and intervention toward greater reliance on market forces; (c) the early restoration of fiscal and monetary discipline; (d) the rehabilitation of the economic and social infrastructure; and (e) the undertaking of structural and institutional reforms to enhance the efficiency of the economy and encourage the expansion of private savings and investment. Ghana's adjustment efforts have been supported by successive arrangements with the IMF, including, since 1988, a three-year arrangement under the enhanced structural adjustment facility (ESAF). Overall, the total amount of IMF financial resources committed to Ghana during 1983–91 amounted to SDR 1,208 million. The World Bank and other creditors and donors have also provided substantial technical and concessional financial assistance.

To improve the allocation of resources and the external payments position, special emphasis has been placed on pursuing a flexible exchange rate policy and liberalizing gradually the exchange and trade system. In particular, the official exchange rate was devalued in several discrete steps from April 1983 through January 1986, while a weekly auction market for foreign exchange was introduced in September 1986. Thereafter, access to the auction was gradually broadened to include by early 1990 all payments and transfers for current international transactions. In addition, the parallel market for foreign exchange was legalized through the establishment in April 1988 of foreign exchange bureaus, licensed to buy and sell foreign

---

[1]For more details, see Beaugrand (1984) and Chand and van Til (1988).

Box 1. Ghana: A Profile

Ghana is a low-income developing country, located on the west coast of Africa, with a population of about 14.4 million and an estimated per capita gross domestic product (GDP) of US$400 in 1990.

Ghana is well endowed with a broad range of natural resources, such as arable land, forests, and sizable deposits of gold, diamonds, bauxite, and manganese, as well as a considerable potential for hydroelectric power. The economy has traditionally depended to a high degree on primary (agricultural as well as mineral) production and exports. Exports of cocoa, gold, and timber still account for the bulk of total merchandise exports, with respective shares of 43 percent, 24 percent, and 11 percent.

Together with forestry and fishing, the agricultural sector employs about two thirds of the labor force and accounts for about half of total output. Agricultural production, which is primarily small scale, is concentrated in cocoa and staple food crops. Ghana ranks among the world's largest producers and exporters of cocoa, even though its relative position has recently dropped from a long-held first place to third, behind Côte d'Ivoire and Brazil. Services comprise the second largest sector in the economy, accounting for an increasing share in real GDP (42 percent in 1990). Finally, the industrial sector, which accounts for the remaining 14 percent of GDP, is relatively diverse and well developed compared with other sub-Saharan African countries.

exchange at freely determined prices. The foreign exchange bureaus and the auction market were finally unified in the context of an interbank market in April 1990, while the outstanding external payments arrears were gradually eliminated by June 1990. The consequent substantial real depreciation of the official exchange rate has made it possible to raise real producer prices for cocoa and other food crops and encourage the diversification of exports. The exchange rate adjustments, together with a restructuring of import tariffs, have also allowed a scaling back of the protective system and the promotion of efficient import substitution. Furthermore, most price controls have been abolished and the remaining administered prices managed flexibly.

The early restoration of fiscal discipline and the pursuit of a growth-oriented fiscal strategy have been integral to the adjustment program. Fiscal policy has been directed at raising government savings and lowering the overall budget deficit, thus allowing, together with the increasing inflows of net foreign financing, a sharp reduction in the Government's recourse to domestic bank financing and, since 1987, sizable net repayments to the banking system. On the revenue side, policies have focused on improving tax administration, broadening the tax base, and rationalizing the structure of taxation. Tax reforms have been aimed at removing the existing distortions and strengthening economic incentives, particularly for private savings and investment, as well as enhancing efficiency and equity in the economy. Tax reforms included reductions in the average personal and corporate income tax rates, the withholding tax on dividends, and the capital gains tax. On the expenditure side, policies have been addressed toward raising capital outlays in the context of a rolling three-year public investment

program, aimed at the rehabilitation of the economic infrastructure, and channeling more resources to operations and maintenance, particularly in the priority sectors of agriculture, health, and education. Moreover, the size of the civil service has been scaled back by the release of redundant employees, while wages and salaries in the government sector have been raised significantly in real terms, and the differentials between the lowest- and highest-paid employees widened to allow the Government to attract and retain qualified staff.

Government revenue and expenditure policies have also been directed toward achieving a more equitable distribution of the benefits and costs of adjustment, aiding in particular the most vulnerable social and economic groups—the small farmers, the urban unemployed and underemployed, and the retrenched public sector employees. In this regard, outlays on education, health, and social welfare services have been raised in the context of the public expenditure program, while a number of small-scale targeted projects, financed by external assistance under the program of actions to mitigate the social costs of adjustment (PAMSCAD), have been implemented since early 1989.

Broadly restrictive monetary and credit policies have been pursued since 1983, designed to achieve the inflation and balance of payments objectives of the program, while allowing the attainment of the targeted expansion in output. Within a tight overall credit policy, a reduction in the Government's recourse to net borrowing from the banking system has facilitated strong increases in real terms in credit to the nongovernment sector. These policies have been accompanied by a gradual lifting of controls on bank deposit and lending interest rates by early 1988 and the abolition of controls on the sectoral allocation of bank credit by late 1987, except for a minimum requirement for lending to the agricultural sector, which was finally abolished in late 1990. In addition, an auction system for issuing treasury bills was introduced in 1987, indicating increased reliance on market-based instruments of monetary policy. In this context, several new financial instruments have been introduced by the Bank of Ghana, sold through weekly auctions to bank and nonbank sectors; the monetary management capacity of the Bank of Ghana has been strengthened; and open market operations have been stepped up, contributing to the absorption of excess liquidity from the economy and a significant increase in money market and bank interest rates to positive levels in real terms by mid-1991.

These policies have been complemented since 1987 by the implementation of a range of structural and institutional reforms designed to strengthen the efficiency of the economy and expand private sector activity. Under the state enterprise reform program, initiated in 1987, several measures have been taken to improve the financial position and efficiency of the state enterprise sector, including the liquidation or divestiture of some 40 enterprises by early 1991, the preparation of rolling three-year corporate plans and annual performance agreements for 13 major state enterprises (accounting for the bulk of the state enterprise sector's assets and employment), and the initiation of measures to improve the autonomy and accountability of state enterprises. Under the financial sector reform program, introduced in 1988, restructuring plans for all the financially distressed commercial and development banks have begun to be implemented; the nonperforming bank assets, including loans to state enterprises and the private sector, have been replaced with Bank of Ghana bonds; and the bank capital adequacy requirements and bank supervision have been strengthened. Furthermore, the Investment Code has been revised and the administrative and institutional framework has begun to be simplified so as to make it more conducive to private investment.

Developments During 1983–91

The implementation of these policies has resulted in a major turnaround in Ghana's overall economic and financial performance since 1983. During the eight-year period to 1991, growth in real GDP recovered, allowing gains in real per capita incomes, inflation declined, and the overall balance of payments position switched from deficit to surpluses, facilitating the elimination of external payments arrears and a buildup of gross official reserves.

In particular, real GDP grew on average by over 5 percent a year, albeit from a low base, compared with an estimated annual rate of population growth of 2.6 percent (Chart 1 and Table 1). The expansion in output, although broadly based, was particularly strong in the industrial sector; the increased availability of imported inputs, the realignment of relative prices, and improvements in real producer prices boosted the expansion of activity in the mining and manufacturing sectors and induced a strong recovery in cocoa production. Real wage earnings also rose, although from initially very depressed levels, particularly for the civil service. The year-on-year inflation rate, as measured by changes in consumer prices, decelerated from 142 percent at the end of 1983 to less than 20 percent by May 1991, although it was subject to wide fluctuations from year to year.

Ghana's external position has improved markedly since 1983. The flexible exchange rate policy and the associated gains in external competitiveness have contributed to an expansion in the volume of exports at an average rate of 10 percent a year during 1983–90, reversing the contraction in the previous two decades (Chart 2 and Table 2). The recovery in output growth, combined with the gradual liberalization of exchange restrictions, boosted the expansion in the volume of imports to an average rate of 10 percent a year. While in real terms the deficit on the external balance on goods and services remained modest, the sharp weakening since 1986 in the world price of cocoa, has contributed to a cumulative deterioration in the terms of trade of 37 percent during the four-year period to 1990 and a concomitant widening in the current account deficit. The impact of the worsening in the terms of trade on the external position has been cushioned in part by exchange rate adjustments and a further tightening of financial policies. Overall, the current account deficit, excluding official transfers, increased from the equivalent of less than 1 percent of GDP in 1983 to over 8 percent by 1990.

The rising external financing requirements have been covered in part by modestly growing inflows of private capital, including direct investment, and more important, by increases in the inflows of official external assistance; the inflows of official grants and long-term concessional loans rose from the equivalent of less than 1 percent of GDP in 1983 to about 10 percent of GDP by 1990, facilitating a build up of gross official reserves and the gradual elimination of external payments arrears. Reflecting prudent external debt management, the outstanding external public debt declined as a ratio

Chart 1. Domestic Economic Indicators

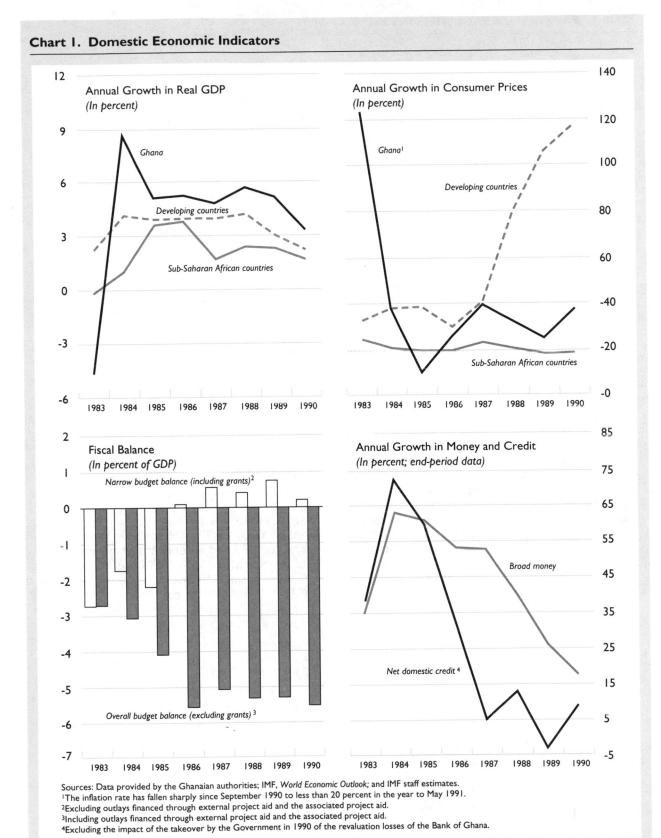

Sources: Data provided by the Ghanaian authorities; IMF, *World Economic Outlook*; and IMF staff estimates.
[1]The inflation rate has fallen sharply since September 1990 to less than 20 percent in the year to May 1991.
[2]Excluding outlays financed through external project aid and the associated project aid.
[3]Including outlays financed through external project aid and the associated project aid.
[4]Excluding the impact of the takeover by the Government in 1990 of the revaluation losses of the Bank of Ghana.

Table 1. Economic and Financial Indicators, 1983–90

	1983	1984	1985	1986	1987	1988	1989	1990
	(Annual percentage change, unless otherwise specified)							
National income and prices								
Real GDP	−4.6	8.6	5.1	5.2	4.8	5.6	5.1	3.3
Real GDP per capita	−7.0	5.9	2.4	2.5	2.1	2.9	2.4	0.6
Nominal GDP (in billions of cedis)	184.0	270.6	343.0	511.4	746.0	1,051.2	1,417.2	1,902.3
Consumer price index (annual average)	122.8	39.7	10.3	24.6	39.8	31.4	25.2	37.2
Consumer price index (end of period)	142.4	6.0	19.5	33.3	34.2	26.6	30.5	35.9
External sector								
Exports, f.o.b.	−27.7	29.1	11.6	18.5	10.0	6.9	−8.2	11.0
Imports, f.o.b.	−15.1	23.3	9.0	9.3	27.3	6.1	1.5	22.6
Terms of trade	6.8	30.2	−5.9	12.5	−8.3	−9.0	−16.2	−9.5
Nominal effective exchange rate	−58.3	−75.4	−27.0	−49.8	−40.4	−17.5	−11.5	−10.5
Real effective exchange rate	−32.8	−61.4	−27.3	−42.5	−22.9	−4.3	−5.8	−0.2
Cedis per U.S. dollar	8.8	36.0	54.4	89.2	153.7	202.3	270.0	326.3
Government budget								
Revenue and grants[1]	94.9	121.1	78.0	82.6	50.8	38.5	39.5	24.6
Total expenditure[2]	65.7	79.9	74.2	53.1	45.9	40.1	36.2	29.3
Current expenditure	70.2	70.7	64.9	58.2	32.5	37.8	33.9	33.3
Capital expenditure[3]	35.3	158.0	126.7	32.5	111.4	47.2	42.8	18.5
Money and credit								
Net domestic assets[4,5]	44.4	84.3	77.1	49.8	11.8	8.5	−10.7	−19.6
Credit to the government[4,5]	67.4	15.2	8.5	4.4	−8.6	−7.4	−7.7	−8.8
Credit to the rest of the economy[4,6]	−22.9	63.1	63.0	35.7	14.4	16.5	6.0	12.6
Broad money	38.1	72.1	59.5	53.7	53.0	43.0	26.9	18.0
Velocity (GDP/average broad money)	10.4	9.7	7.5	7.6	7.2	7.0	7.0	7.7
	(In percent of GDP)							
Investment and savings								
Gross investment	3.7	6.9	9.6	9.7	13.4	14.2	15.5	16.0
Gross national savings	3.0	5.9	7.1	8.2	11.3	12.5	13.7	11.6
Government budget								
Surplus or deficit (−)[2]	−2.7	−1.8	−2.2	0.1	0.5	0.4	0.7	0.2
Overall surplus or deficit (−)[7]	−2.7	−2.3	−3.0	−3.3	−2.4	−2.8	−2.1	−2.4
Revenue and grants	5.6	8.4	11.8	14.4	14.9	14.6	15.1	14.1
Total expenditure[2]	8.3	10.2	14.0	14.3	14.3	14.3	14.4	13.9
External sector								
Current account balance[8]	−0.8	−1.0	−2.5	−1.5	−2.1	−1.7	−1.8	4.4
External debt outstanding[9]	9.7	26.4	34.1	46.5	63.7	58.0	55.2	52.6
Debt service	0.7	3.3	5.8	6.7	10.8	12.5	9.8	6.4
	(In percent of exports of goods and services)							
External debt service								
Including the Fund	31.9	40.4	54.7	47.8	58.3	68.0	58.1	37.9
Excluding the Fund	27.7	36.1	46.9	36.9	31.8	34.0	32.5	22.5
	(In millions of U.S. dollars)							
Current account balance[8]	−157.6	−75.3	−156.7	−84.8	−101.9	−89.5	−95.0	−256.0
Overall balance of payments	−243.0	37.2	−115.5	−56.8	138.5	124.6	127.4	85.0
Gross international reserves								
(End of period)	184.6	131.8	145.2	148.7	193.6	200.8	249.0	269.3
(Equivalent months of imports c.i.f.)	4.6	2.4	2.4	2.2	2.2	2.2	2.7	2.4

Sources: Data provided by the Ghanaian authorities; and IMF staff estimates.
[1] Excluding project-related grants.
[2] Excluding capital outlays financed through external project aid.
[3] Including net lending and, from 1987 onward, the special efficiency program.
[4] In percent of broad money at the beginning of the period.
[5] Excluding the takeover by the Government in 1990 of the accumulated valuation losses of the Bank of Ghana.
[6] Including financing of the Cocoa Board's operations, but excluding other items (net).
[7] Including capital expenditure financed through external project aid.
[8] Including official grants.
[9] End period data; including debt to the IMF.

Chart 2. External Economic Indicators

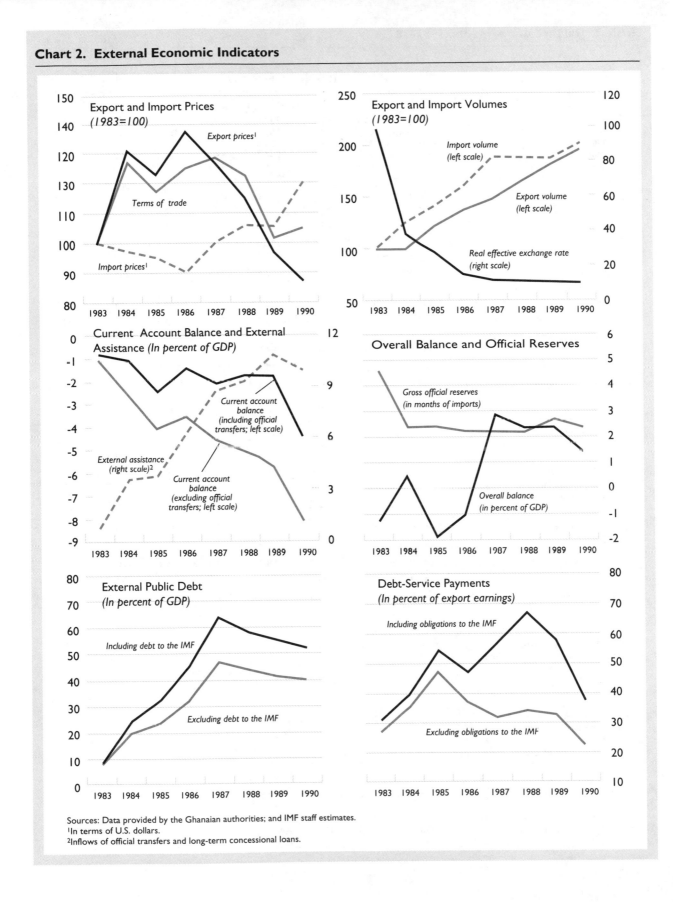

Sources: Data provided by the Ghanaian authorities; and IMF staff estimates.
[1]In terms of U.S. dollars.
[2]Inflows of official transfers and long-term concessional loans.

Table 2. Balance of Payments, 1983–90

	1983	1984	1985	1986	1987	1988	1989	1990
				(In millions of U.S. dollars)				
Exports, f.o.b.	439.1	566.7	632.3	749.4	824.0	881.0	808.3	896.9
Cocoa beans and products	268.6	381.7	412.0	503.3	495.4	462.0	407.8	360.6
Gold	114.1	103.3	90.6	106.4	139.8	168.5	159.9	201.7
Timber	14.7	21.2	27.8	44.1	89.8	106.2	80.2	118.0
Other	41.7	60.5	101.9	95.6	99.0	144.2	160.4	216.6
Imports, f.o.b.	499.7	616.0	671.3	733.5	933.8	990.9	1,006.0	1,233.7
Oil	161.1	161.0	209.5	122.6	141.1	142.9	155.8	199.9
Non-oil	338.6	455.0	461.8	610.9	792.7	848.0	850.2	1,033.8
Trade balance	−60.6	−49.3	−39.0	15.9	−109.8	−110.0	−197.7	−336.8
Services (net)	−186.0	−229.2	−254.4	−290.9	−315.9	−326.8	−318.8	−345.0
Of which: interest	(−81.3)	(−101.0)	(−102.9)	(−101.2)	(−121.6)	(−126.6)	(−109.2)	(−106.7)
Private unrequited transfers (net)	16.6	73.5	31.9	72.1	201.6	172.4	202.1	201.9
Current account balance, excluding net official transfers	−230.0	−205.0	−261.5	−202.9	−224.1	−264.4	−314.4	−479.9
Official unrequited transfers (net)	72.4	129.7	104.6	118.2	122.2	174.9	219.4	223.9
Current account balance, including net official transfers	−157.6	−75.3	−156.9	−84.7	−101.9	−89.5	−95.0	−256.0
Capital account	102.0	93.3	62.4	20.0	255.0	217.8	222.4	341.0
Official capital (net)	27.7	186.7	32.1	123.1	217.9	187.2	192.0	275.8
Long-term loans	15.0	83.6	109.8	226.5	267.3	273.0	307.0	316.8
Inflows	84.4	133.4	134.8	256.7	303.7	307.5	343.9	348.9
Amortization	−69.4	−49.8	−25.0	−30.2	−36.4	−34.5	−36.9	−32.1
Medium-term loans	12.7	104.3	−70.3	−92.2	−36.9	−72.7	−103.9	−37.5
Inflows	67.8	169.5	152.5	128.2	109.0	101.6	34.1	65.3
Amortization	−55.1	−65.2	−222.8	−220.4	−145.9	−174.3	−138.0	−102.8
Trust fund	—	−1.2	−7.4	−11.2	−12.4	−13.1	−11.1	−3.5
Private capital (net)	13.4	−8.7	5.8	7.0	1.7	4.0	11.7	52.8
Direct investment	1.6	2.0	5.6	4.3	4.7	5.0	15.0	14.8
Other	11.8	−10.7	0.2	2.7	−3.0	−1.0	−3.3	38.0
Short-term capital	60.9	−84.7	24.5	−110.1	35.4	26.6	18.7	12.4
Errors and omissions	−187.4	19.2	−21.0	7.9	−14.6	−3.8	—	—
Overall balance	−243.0	37.2	−115.5	−56.7	138.5	124.6	127.4	85.0
Financing	243.0	−37.2	115.5	56.8	−137.9	−126.2	−127.4	−85.0
Change in net foreign assets	241.9	−26.9	107.7	66.2	−131.4	−124.8	−142.2	−102.0
IMF transactions (net)	258.7	213.7	122.0	16.1	−25.2	−45.5	4.4	−47.7
Change in arrears (reduction −)	−33.7	−207.8	−56.7	−3.7	−71.6	−34.8	−47.7	−17.3
Other reserves (increase −)	16.9	−32.8	42.4	53.7	−34.6	−44.5	−98.9	−37.0
Bilateral payments agreements	1.1	−10.3	7.8	−9.4	−6.5	−1.4	14.8	17.0
				(In percent; unless otherwise indicated)				
Memorandum items:								
Current account deficit (−) In percent of GDP Including official transfers	−0.8	−1.0	−2.5	−1.5	−2.1	−1.7	−1.8	−4.4
Excluding official transfers	−1.1	−2.7	−4.1	−3.5	−4.6	−5.1	−6.0	−8.2
Exports as a ratio to GDP	2.1	7.5	10.0	13.1	17.0	17.0	15.4	15.4
Imports as a ratio to GDP	2.4	8.2	10.6	12.8	19.2	19.1	19.2	21.2
Cocoa exports (beans) Volume (in thousands of tons)	159,280.0	149,574.0	171,747.0	195,224.0	197,988.0	200,904.0	255,860.0	247,380.0
Price (in US$ per ton)	1,520.0	2,351.3	2,189.1	2,406.5	2,278.0	2,101.8	1,490.3	1,309.0

Sources: Data provided by the Ghanaian authorities; and IMF staff estimates.

to GDP from a peak of 64 percent in 1987 to 53 percent by 1990, while its maturity structure and terms have improved; as a result, the debt service ratio, including obligations to the Fund, eased to 38 percent by 1990.

Barring unforeseen developments, Ghana's external position is expected to improve further over the medium and long term, even on the assumption of no significant reversal of the terms of trade losses, consistent with a reduced reliance on external assistance. The volume of exports is expected to grow at a rate higher than that for the volume of imports. The volume of gold exports, Ghana's second largest source of foreign exchange, is expected to increase sharply in the period ahead, reflecting the coming on stream of a number of new mining ventures, the rehabilitation of existing mines, and the encouragement of small-scale mining. Timber exports and nontraditional exports are also expected to expand. Overall, the current account deficit as a ratio to GDP and the debt service ratio are both expected to decline over the medium term.

Despite the improvement in its economic and financial performance, Ghana continues to be confronted with a number of structural, institutional, and financial constraints. These constraints include a still high inflation rate, a small though developing private sector, levels of domestic savings and investment that are still too low to allow a self-sustained growth in output, notwithstanding the progress made in this regard in recent years, and increasing pressure on the public sector's management and implementation capacity.

III   Growth, Savings, and Investment

Ghana's adjustment efforts since 1983 have resulted in a recovery in output and an expansion in gross national savings and investment, albeit from historically low levels. The recovery in activity was pronounced in the industrial and services sectors, benefiting from the emphasis of policies on rehabilitating and expanding the basic economic infrastructure, restoring an appropriate exchange rate, liberalizing the exchange system, removing the distortions in the structure of relative prices, reforming the tax system, and restoring and maintaining macroeconomic stability.

These policies contributed also to the increase in savings and investment. The recovery in total savings and investment in the economy has emanated mainly from the public sector. The private sector's response to a better macroeconomic environment was initially slow, as it could have been expected after a prolonged period of economic dislocation, but picked up in later years. This response has been aided by the initiation of structural and institutional reforms, particularly in the state enterprise and financial sectors, although much more remains to be done. Overall, while progress has been made since 1983, domestic savings and investment in Ghana have not yet reached the levels required to sustain a satisfactory rate of economic growth and generate adequate new employment opportunities for Ghana's rapidly growing labor force. In view of this, the policies currently in place are aimed at removing the remaining impediments to a vigorous expansion in private sector activity in all sectors of the economy, while strengthening further government finances and scaling back the size of the public sector.

Recent Developments

After a cumulative decline of about 15 percent from the early 1970s to 1983, real GDP expanded at an annual average rate of 5.4 percent during the seven-year period to 1990, resulting in sizable gains in real per capita incomes (Chart 3 and Table 3). The combination of inappropriate economic policies and exogenous domestic and external shocks during 1971–83 had led to cumulative declines of the order of 50–60 percent in the real value added in the cocoa, mining, manufacturing, and construction sectors, as well as contractions of about 35 percent in real activity in the wholesale and retail trade sectors. Since the introduction of the economic recovery program in 1983, Ghana's growth performance has compared very favorably with that of other sub-Saharan African countries and all developing countries in general.

The fastest growing sectors since 1983 have been the industrial and services sectors, while the growth of activity in the agricultural sector has been weaker, keeping barely in line with population growth. The increases in real producer prices for cocoa and other food crops contributed to an expansion in production, but the vagaries in weather conditions continued to induce fluctuations in agricultural output from year to year. Nonetheless, by 1990 the level of real value added in the cocoa sector was still less than half its peak in 1972. Activity in the industrial sector was boosted by the removal of price distortions, the increased availability of foreign exchange and imported inputs, and an interest expressed by foreign investors in Ghana's mining sector. Between 1983 and 1990, the volume of gold and total mining production increased by over 60 percent, while manufacturing output increased by about 80 percent. The more favorable macroeconomic environment benefited also the services sector. Activity in the transport and trade sectors, which are key for the marketing of agricultural and manufacturing output and employ a large part of the urban labor force, recorded a sustained growth throughout the period.

As a result of the differentiated growth rates recorded in the various sectors of economic activity, the structural composition of total real GDP has changed markedly. The most important change has been a continuation of the upward trend in the share of value added in the services sector in total GDP. This share rose from 38 percent in 1983 (28 percent in 1971) to 44 percent by 1990, owing essentially to the growth of the trade sector; during

Chart 3. Developments in Output

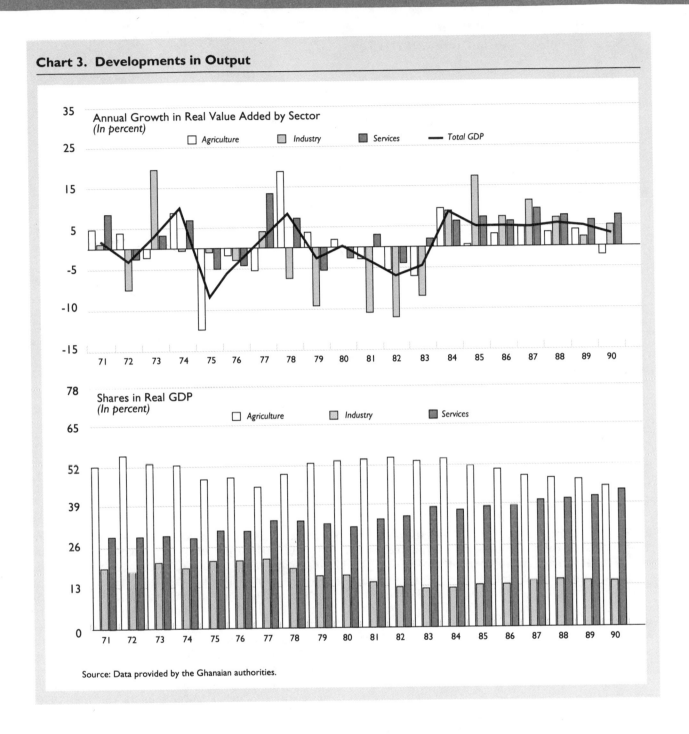

Source: Data provided by the Ghanaian authorities.

the 1970s, the expansion in the share of the services sector emanated largely from government services. The second major change was a partial reversal of the earlier decline in the share of the industrial sector. After having fallen from 19 percent in 1971 to less than 12 percent in 1983, the share of value added in the industrial sector in total GDP rose to over 14 percent by 1990. The share of the mining sector remained modest, at just over 1 percent, notwithstanding the fact that mineral exports accounted in 1990 for 27 percent of total export earnings, while the share of manufacturing rose to 9 percent. The counterpart of these developments was a decline in the share of agricultural output from 53 percent in 1983 to 45 percent in 1990, reflecting a contraction of the share of food production and a small further decline in the share of the cocoa sector. The latter

Table 3. Developments in Output, 1971–90
(In percent)

	1971–83		1983–90		1971	1983	1990
	Cumulative change	Annual average growth	Cumulative change	Annual average growth	(Shares in real GDP)		
Agriculture, forestry, and fishing	−10.8	−0.9	20.9	2.7	50.5	53.4	44.7
Agriculture and livestock	12.7	1.0	21.1	2.8	27.8	37.1	31.2
Cocoa	−59.7	−7.3	26.1	3.4	16.3	7.8	6.8
Forestry and logging	14.0	1.1	13.1	1.8	4.8	6.5	5.1
Fishing	4.5	0.4	20.7	2.7	1.6	1.9	1.6
Industrial production	−47.5	−5.2	78.0	8.6	18.6	11.6	14.3
Mining and quarrying	−60.9	−7.5	73.8	8.2	2.4	1.1	1.3
Manufacturing	−48.5	−5.4	89.1	9.5	11.3	6.9	9.1
Electricity, water, and gas	141.2	7.6	112.0	11.3	0.3	0.9	1.3
Construction	−50.4	−5.7	40.6	5.0	4.6	2.7	2.6
Services	12.9	1.0	65.7	7.5	28.3	37.9	43.5
Transport, storage, and communications	8.5	0.7	91.0	9.7	3.1	4.0	5.4
Wholesale and retail trade	−34.6	−3.5	109.1	11.1	12.6	9.7	14.1
Finance, insurance, and business services	34.7	2.5	51.4	6.1	5.5	8.7	9.2
Government and other	82.5	5.1	39.7	4.9	7.1	15.3	14.8
Sub-total	−10.9	−1.0	43.8	5.3	97.4	102.8	102.5
minus: imputed bank charges	168.2	8.6	54.2	6.4	1.2	3.7	4.0
plus: import duties	−79.4	−12.3	127.0	12.4	3.8	0.9	1.5
Gross domestic product	−15.6	−1.4	44.2	5.4	100.0	100.0	100.0

Sources: Statistical Service, Accra; and IMF staff estimates.

fell from 8 percent to 7 percent, respectively, even though cocoa exports continue to provide the bulk of total export proceeds (40 percent in 1990).

Gross national investment rose in relation to GDP from a historically low level of 3.7 percent in 1983 to an estimated 16.0 percent in 1990 (Chart 4 and Table 4).[2,3] Notwithstanding this progress, Ghana's investment ratio in 1990 was only slightly higher than in the early 1970s and lower than the average for all sub-Saharan African countries (about 19 percent) and all African countries (about 20 percent). The higher levels of investment were financed primarily by increased gross national savings and, to a lesser extent, by higher reliance on foreign savings (as measured by the external current account deficit including official transfers). In particular, gross national savings rose from the equivalent of 3.5 percent of GDP in 1983 to 13.0 percent in 1989, before easing to an estimated 11.6 percent of GDP in 1990. At this level, Ghana's gross national savings ratio in 1990 was still somewhat lower than in the mid-1970s and lower than the average for all sub-Saharan African countries (about 13 percent) and all African countries (17 percent).[4] The use of foreign savings, on the other hand, rose steadily from 0.8 percent of GDP in 1983 to 4.4 percent by 1990.

The increase in the investment to GDP ratio since 1983 reflects largely an expansion in public investment, including the investment of state enterprises financed under the public investment pro-

[2]Ghana's savings and investment balances are based on IMF staff estimates, derived from the available official national accounts statistics. The national accounts statistics, particularly on the expenditure side, are subject to a large margin of error.

[3]The movements in the nominal investment to GDP ratio exaggerate the decline in the volume of investment during 1970–83 and overstate the increase during 1983–90, as a result of the recorded changes in the relative prices of investment goods. As the bulk of investment goods are imported, the overvaluation of the cedi during the period to 1983 had resulted in a sharp moderation in the growth of the investment deflator relative to the growth in the GDP deflator, while with the exchange rate adjustments in the period after 1983 the investment deflator grew much faster than the GDP deflator.

[4]For a review of recent developments in savings in developing countries, see Aghevli and others (1990) and IMF (1991).

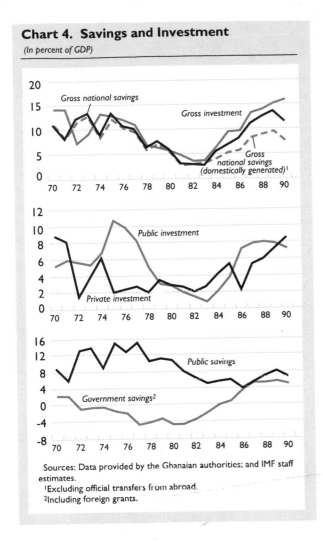

Chart 4. Savings and Investment
(In percent of GDP)

Gross national savings

Gross investment

Gross national savings (domestically generated)[1]

Public investment

Private investment

Public savings

Government savings[2]

Sources: Data provided by the Ghanaian authorities; and IMF staff estimates.
[1]Excluding official transfers from abroad.
[2]Including foreign grants.

of electricity and the improvements in the transportation network and other basic economic infrastructure, as well as the wider availability of foreign exchange and the gradual removal of the exchange and trade restrictions, paved the way for a recovery in private investment. Private investment stabilized at about 4 percent of GDP during 1983–87, but expanded to an estimated 9 percent by 1990, including a sizable increase in foreign direct investment in the gold mining sector.

The predominance of public investment and its emphasis on the rehabilitation of the basic economic infrastructure were reflected in the composition of total investment. The share of buildings and other construction works in total gross fixed investment (in constant prices) amounted on average to over 50 percent during 1983–88, while the share of machinery and equipment remained at less than 25 percent. Estimates by the Statistical Service of Ghana indicate that more than half of real gross fixed investment since 1983 represented capital depreciation. As a result, Ghana's real capital stock in most sectors of the economy has risen only marginally over this period. Notable exceptions were the mining and cocoa sectors; productive capacity in the gold mining sector increased sharply, while the higher real cocoa producer prices induced plantings of saplings and a more efficient exploitation of existing cocoa trees. Overall, the expansion in real GDP was facilitated by increasing rates of utilization of existing idle capacity in both the industrial and agricultural sectors, and a strong growth in low capital intensity service activities.

The improvement in government finances since 1983 has also allowed the Government to contribute to the expansion in gross national savings. With the recovery in tax receipts, more foreign grants, and the containment of the pressure on current expenditure, the current balance of the government budget (used as an approximation of the Government's savings position) shifted from dissavings equivalent to 2 percent of GDP in 1983 to savings of almost 6 percent of GDP in 1989, before easing to 5 percent in 1990. The resumption of growth in real private disposable incomes allowed a gradual increase in the private savings ratio. Private savings rose from 5 percent of GDP in 1983 to almost 7 percent by 1990, though subject to sizable fluctuations from year to year.

The expansion in total gross national savings since 1983, and in particular the gains in government savings, have benefited from large inflows of external grants provided by foreign donors in support of Ghana's adjustment efforts; these grants rose from negligible levels in 1983 to 4 percent of GDP by 1990. Excluding official grants, domestic

gram. Public investment rose from a mere 1 percent of GDP in 1983 to 8 percent by 1988, but eased somewhat to an estimated 7 percent of GDP in 1990.[5] The strong recovery of public investment reflected the emphasis of Ghana's reform efforts on the rehabilitation and expansion of the productive capacity of the country after several years of neglect, as well as the importance attached by the authorities to improving the social infrastructure, particularly in the areas of education and health. The restoration of a normal supply

---

[5]The estimates for public sector investment and savings balances are based on fiscal data, which are expressed in cash terms. It is assumed that such data provide a reasonably good estimate of government savings and public investment on a national accounts basis; private savings and investment are derived as a residual. In view of these approximations, these data provide a rough order of magnitude of sectoral savings and investment balances and they should therefore be interpreted with caution.

Table 4. Savings and Investment, 1970–90
(In percent of GDP)

	1970	1975	1980	1983	1984	1985	1986	1987	1988	1989	1990
Gross disposable national income	97.8	100.2	100.1	100.3	101.4	100.5	102.0	104.4	104.1	105.8	105.4
Total consumption	86.6	86.3	95.1	96.7	93.4	92.4	92.0	92.8	91.7	92.1	93.8
Private consumption	73.7	73.3	83.9	90.8	86.1	83.0	80.9	82.8	81.7	82.9	84.9
Government consumption	12.8	13.0	11.2	5.9	7.3	9.4	11.1	10.0	10.0	9.2	8.9
Gross national savings[1]	11.2	13.8	5.0	3.6	8.0	8.1	10.0	11.7	12.5	13.7	11.6
Of which: domestically generated[2]	10.8	13.4	4.5	3.3	6.2	6.5	8.0	9.1	9.1	9.5	7.8
Private savings	8.9	15.6	9.9	5.4	7.8	7.0	6.1	6.1	7.2	8.1	6.7
Government savings[3]	2.3	−1.8	−4.9	−1.8	0.1	1.1	4.0	5.5	5.2	5.6	4.9
Gross investment	14.1	12.7	5.6	3.7	6.9	9.6	9.7	13.4	14.2	15.5	16.0
Public investment	5.3	10.7	2.8	0.9	2.5	4.2	7.3	7.9	8.0	7.8	7.3
Private investment	8.8	2.1	2.9	2.9	4.4	5.4	2.4	5.5	6.2	7.7	8.7
Statistical discrepancy[4]	−0.1	−0.7	0.8	−0.6	−2.1	−1.0	−1.8	−0.4	—	—	—
Gross national savings, adjusted for statistical discrepancy	11.1	13.1	5.8	3.0	5.9	7.1	8.2	11.3	12.5	13.7	11.6
Of which: domestically generated	10.7	12.7	5.3	2.6	4.2	5.4	6.1	8.8	9.1	9.5	7.8
Public sector financial balance	−3.0	−12.5	−7.6	−2.7	−2.3	−3.0	−3.3	−2.4	−2.8	−2.2	−2.4
Government savings[3]	2.3	−1.8	−4.9	−1.8	0.1	1.1	4.0	5.5	5.2	5.6	4.9
Public investment	5.3	10.7	2.8	0.9	2.5	4.2	7.3	7.9	8.0	7.8	7.3
Private sector financial balance	0.0	12.9	7.8	1.9	1.3	0.5	1.8	0.3	1.1	0.4	−2.0
Private savings (including statistical discrepancy)	8.8	14.9	10.7	4.8	5.7	5.9	4.2	5.8	7.3	8.1	6.7
Private investment	8.8	2.1	2.9	2.9	4.4	5.4	2.4	5.5	6.2	7.7	8.7
External current account balance	−3.1	0.4	0.2	−0.8	−1.0	−2.5	−1.5	−2.1	−1.7	−1.8	−4.4

Sources: Statistical Service, Accra; and IMF staff estimates.

[1] Defined as gross national disposable income minus total consumption.

[2] Gross national savings minus external official transfers.

[3] Central Government current budget deficit; the latter is estimated as total revenue and grants (broad coverage) minus current expenditure and special efficiency.

[4] Discrepancy between the national accounts estimates of external balance on goods and nonfactor services, net factor payments, and transfers, and the balance of payments estimate of the current account balance.

savings, which are perhaps more indicative of the gains from Ghana's adjustment policies, increased from 3 percent of GDP in 1983 to almost 10 percent in 1989, but fell back in 1990 to an estimated 8 percent of GDP.

The weakening in the savings performance in 1990 reflected a slowdown in the growth in real national disposable income, adjusted for the losses in the terms of trade, in the face of an estimated strong growth in private consumption, and in part

the adverse impact of special factors on government finances (see Section V). The terms of trade deteriorated by 10 percent in 1990, after a cumulative worsening in the previous three years of 30 percent, largely as a result of a decline in cocoa prices in world markets. The impact of the terms of trade losses prior to 1990 on domestically generated savings, as recorded in the national accounts statistics, appears to have been cushioned by the return into the formal markets of previously unrecorded parallel market activities, such as cross-border sales of cocoa. The reintegration of these transactions into the formal sector of the economy has raised both estimated real GDP and private incomes.

Financial Balances

The public sector's net financial balance, estimated as the difference between government savings and public investment, deteriorated during most of the 1970s, as public investment expanded despite the increasing government dissavings (Table 4). The resulting pressures on government finances and the rapidly eroding tax base necessitated cuts in public investment in the early 1980s, which narrowed the net financial deficit of the public sector. Over the same period, in the face of declining real GDP and a binding foreign exchange constraint, private investment fell as a ratio to GDP faster than private savings. Thus, the net financial surplus of the private sector virtually covered the net financial deficit of the public sector, containing the external current account deficit (including official transfers) to modest levels in relation to GDP. Higher access to foreign savings during this period was constrained by given Ghana's inappropriate domestic policies.

With the reorientation of Ghana's economic and financial policies since 1983 and the associated relaxation of the external constraints, the vicious circle of declining savings and investment was quickly reversed. Government savings have expanded more or less in line with public sector investment, keeping the public sector's net financial deficit low, averaging less than 3 percent of GDP. The net financial surplus of the private sector, on the other hand, declined gradually from 2 percent of GDP in 1983 to virtually zero by 1989; private investment over this period rose slightly faster than private savings. In 1990, however, it is estimated that private savings fell as a ratio to GDP, while private investment rose further, shifting the private sector's net financial balance into a deficit equivalent to 2 percent of GDP. As a result, the external current account deficit fluctuated at around 2 percent of GDP during 1983–89, but widened in 1990 to 4.4 percent of GDP. Overall, the counterpart to the reliance on foreign savings during 1983–90 was a faster expansion in total investment than in total national savings in the economy. The widening external current account imbalances over this period have been covered primarily by larger inflows of long-term concessional loans from bilateral and multilateral creditors in support of Ghana's structural and financial reforms.

Private Sector Response

The private sector in Ghana has responded positively to the improvement in the macroeconomic environment since 1983, the restoration of an appropriate exchange rate and the associated marked gains in external competitiveness, the strengthening in economic incentives, and the structural and institutional reforms initiated by the Government. This response was initially rather slow, but picked up in subsequent years.

Overall, the speed and strength of the private sector response so far have not been fully satisfactory, reflecting perhaps the initial very poor state of the economy and the time needed to rebuild confidence in the sustainability of new policies and in the outlook for the economy. The protracted economic decline prior to 1983 had left the private sector in Ghana in a state of virtual devastation from which it was difficult to recover within a short time. Real wage earnings and other private incomes had fallen sharply to levels barely covering the basic needs of the population; agricultural incomes and domestic food supply had been particularly affected by the droughts of 1975–77 and 1981–83. Private businesses, on the other hand, had been disrupted by the acute shortages of imported inputs and spare parts, the proliferation of direct government controls, and the steep decline in real aggregate demand in the economy, resulting in low rates of capacity utilization, poor maintenance of the capital stock, and the emergence of financial imbalances for the business sector. Starting from this weak financial position, many private enterprises found it difficult to adapt to the adjustments in the exchange rate and other relative prices in the economy, notwithstanding the new profitable business opportunities opened to them. As a result of the policy reforms, several private and state enterprises that in the past had been sheltered from domestic and foreign competition were unavoidably forced to rationalize their operations or ultimately to go out of business.

The recovery in real GDP growth following the inception of the economic recovery program in 1983 allowed for the first time in two decades sustained gains in real private national disposable income per capita of about 2.8 percent a year. These gains have permitted an expansion in real private consumption expenditure of about 2.5 percent a year and an improvement in private savings, both in real terms and as a ratio to GDP. A number of institutional and structural constraints may have restrained an even stronger response of private savings. First, the high rate of population growth limited the expansion in real per capita incomes; the actual rate of increase in the population is officially estimated at 2.6 percent a year. Second, the low level of confidence in the banking system by the public at large, combined with the negative real interest rates on bank deposits that have prevailed virtually throughout the period since 1983, discouraged the expansion of financial savings; these problems were exacerbated by the high time costs involved in depositing and withdrawing money from commercial banks and, until recently, the limited range of financial instruments available to private investors.[6] Finally, high inflation during this period, even though it was lower than in the early 1980s, may have contributed to the hoarding of durable consumer goods as a hedge.

Similarly, a more vigorous response of private investment in sectors other than gold mining and cocoa appears to have been impeded by a number of institutional, structural, and financial constraints, inherent to Ghana's present stage of economic development. In particular, the dearth of medium-term financing, the rudimentary state of the capital market, and weaknesses in financial intermediation in general made it difficult for private businesses to find means of financing other than short-term bank credit. The generally low profitability of many private firms and the low overall level of domestic savings limited the prospects for investment financing from their own resources. These difficulties were compounded by the complexity and limited transparency of the legal and administrative framework. Finally, distortions in the tax treatment of capital and investment income, particularly the high capital gains tax (until 1990) and the withholding tax on dividends, acted as a disincentive to new investment and mergers and acquisitions and may have retarded the necessary restructuring of many private enterprises.

With a view to eliminating, or at least alleviating, these constraints, a number of policy actions have been taken or are being implemented since 1990. In particular, the budget for 1991 provided for a major reform of the taxation of capital and investment income, including a reduction from 45 percent to 35 percent in the corporate tax rate applicable to agriculture, manufacturing, real estate, construction, and services; a reduction in the capital gains tax rate to 5 percent, with an exemption from capital gains tax of income from publicly traded companies as well as from mergers and acquisitions; a reduction in the withholding tax on dividends from 30 percent to 15 percent; and an extension of the capital allowances provided under the Investment Code to all enterprises in the manufacturing sector. In addition, restructuring plans for all the banks facing financial difficulties have begun to be implemented; the nonperforming bank assets have been replaced with Bank of Ghana bonds; a stock exchange was introduced in November 1990; the state enterprise divestiture program has been stepped up, with more than 40 enterprises divested by early 1991; and measures are being taken to streamline government regulations and administrative requirements relating inter alia to business registration, the issuance of manufacturing licenses, the restrictions on foreign ownership, technology transfer, tax administration, and labor laws. In the latter regard, in early 1991 an advisory group was set up, whose chairman and the majority of members are from the private sector, to review and make proposals for appropriate changes in the existing laws and administrative requirements to make them consistent with the liberalizing and deregulating thrust of the policy reforms pursued by the Government.

---

[6]Although the empirical evidence suggests that interest rate policies have small effects on savings rates, maintenance of negative real interest rates for prolonged periods could lead to a flight out of financial deposits. For a review of interest rate policies in developing countries, see IMF (1983) and Aghevli and others (1990).

IV Exchange Rate Policy and Exchange Reform

Among the various developing countries that reoriented their exchange rate strategy and began implementing a reform of their exchange rate system during the 1980s, Ghana followed an original and reasonably successful path. With a view to redirecting incentives toward productive activities and exports, and to endowing Ghana with an efficient exchange rate system, a four-stage reform was implemented after the inception of the economic recovery program in April 1983. During the first stage, the massive initial over-valuation of the cedi was corrected through a series of sizable discrete exchange rate adjustments, accompanied by the pursuit of more appropriate fiscal and credit policies. In the second phase, an auction market was established with a view to allowing the cedi's exchange rate to be determined by market forces. During the third stage, which overlapped the second one, the parallel market for foreign exchange was absorbed, largely through the legalization of the foreign exchange bureaus. In the fourth and final phase, which began in early 1990, the unification of the exchange rate system was achieved in the context of a composite auction/interbank arrangement.

Devaluations Under a Pegged Exchange Rate Regime

A series of discrete devaluations was implemented during the initial phase of Ghana's adjustment efforts to correct the overvaluation of the cedi and to remedy the acute foreign exchange crisis that had been brought about, inter alia, by the previous rigidity in the nominal exchange rate of the cedi. Although they did not entirely correct the overvaluation of the currency, the measures adopted during this period were instrumental in ameliorating the severe exchange rate distortions present at the inception of the program and in minimizing the exchange rate adjustment that was to result from the establishment of an auction for foreign exchange. Moreover, this strategy provided time to implement the necessary fiscal and monetary adjustments and to begin rehabilitating the productive base of the economy.

From August 1978 until April 1983, the exchange rate of the cedi was pegged to the U.S. dollar and maintained at 2.75 cedis per U.S. dollar. Since Ghana's inflation rate substantially exceeded average price changes in partner countries during the same period, the real effective exchange rate of the cedi appreciated by 445 percent. Given the concurrent broadening of the imbalance between demand and supply of foreign exchange in the official channels, the differential between the official and the parallel market exchange rates (expressed as a percentage of the official rate) widened considerably, reaching some 2,100 percent in 1982. As the differential between the official and the parallel market exchange rates grew and the balance of payments difficulties worsened, the informal market came to play a dominant role in allocating foreign exchange. Exports plummeted and official exchange channels were increasingly bypassed, which exacerbated the prevailing foreign exchange crisis. Although parallel markets were thriving, there was a general scarcity of imports involving not only consumer goods but also inputs essential to the industrial and agricultural sectors. External sources of financing dried up as debt service obligations were not met. Accordingly, before adopting a more flexible exchange rate policy in the context of an IMF-supported program, Ghana's economy, like a number of other developing countries, was characterized by severe and protracted balance of payments difficulties that included sizable external payments arrears.[7]

Prior to 1983, the authorities had long postponed the introduction of the required policy measures for fear that a large adjustment in the exchange rate would prompt political unrest. Instead, they had attempted to address their balance of

---

[7]By mid-1983, Ghana's external payments arrears amounted to about US$580 million, equivalent to more than 10 percent of GDP and about 18 months of exports.

payments difficulties by resorting to ad hoc restrictions on trade and payments, but such palliatives proved largely ineffective and even detrimental as they fueled further activity in the parallel markets.

As a central element of the economic recovery program, a more realistic exchange rate policy was adopted and the cedi was devalued in stages from 2.75 cedis per U.S. dollar in April 1983 to 90 cedis per U.S. dollar by January 1986. The new exchange rate policy was launched with the establishment in April 1983, as a transitional device, of a scheme of bonuses on foreign exchange receipts and surcharges on foreign exchange payments. The operation of the new scheme resulted in a multiple exchange rate system as two different rates were applied to specified external current receipts and payments. These rates yielded a weighted average rate of 24.7 cedis per U.S. dollar, implying a depreciation of 89 percent in U.S. dollar terms (or 798 percent in local currency terms). In real terms, the resulting exchange rate was close to what it had been in 1972, the last year when the overall balance of payments had been considered broadly sustainable.

Following the initial devaluation, a real exchange rate rule was adopted for the 1983–84 period, with a view to preventing the reemergence of a severe misalignment in relative prices and thereby avoiding a weakening in Ghana's balance of payments position. Under this rule, the exchange rates were to be adjusted quarterly, so that the weighted average exchange rate would move in accordance with an index measuring the inflation differential between Ghana and its main trading partners.

As it became rapidly evident that the system of bonuses and surcharges was excessively cumbersome, this transitory arrangement was terminated on October 10, 1983, and exchange rates in the official system were unified at 30 cedis per U.S. dollar, resulting in a devaluation of about 91 percent in U.S. dollar terms. Subsequently, the exchange rate of the cedi was adjusted periodically in line with the real exchange rate rule. Nonetheless, by the end of 1984 the exchange rate was still considered overvalued, and further action appeared necessary to reach an exchange rate that would help attain the authorities' balance of payments and fiscal targets. Accordingly, beginning with the devaluation effected on December 3, 1984, the exchange rate was adjusted periodically to effect a further significant real effective depreciation. By the end of January 1986, when the last discrete adjustment in the official exchange rate took place before the establishment of an auction, the exchange rate of the cedi had been brought to 90 cedis per U.S. dollar.

During this phase of Ghana's adjustment strategy, the parallel market premium remained substantial, reflecting in part the rationing of foreign exchange in the official banking system for the importation of consumer goods. Imports remained controlled within the framework of an annual import program. Until October 1986, Ghana's import licensing system involved two different import licenses, namely, the Specific Import Licenses and the Special Import Licenses.[8] Pending more radical reforms, the Special Import Licenses scheme was streamlined and liberalized in 1985 when the positive list that limited the range of goods that could be imported under this scheme was replaced by a short negative list, with all goods not explicitly mentioned being deemed freely importable. As a result, there were virtually no quantitative restrictions on imports of goods into Ghana, but only restrictions on importers' access to foreign exchange from the banking system. Under this system, most consumer goods, as well as a number of intermediate and capital goods, could not be financed through purchase of foreign exchange from the banking system (i.e., at the official rate), but had to be financed through alternative sources, at the exchange rate prevailing in the parallel market.

In summary, Ghana effected a series of large devaluations, through which progress was made toward correcting the severe overvaluation of the cedi that prevailed prior to the launching of the economic recovery program. However, the pegged exchange rate arrangement and the series of devaluations that were implemented did not prove sufficient to reach an appropriate exchange rate. By mid-1986, the cedi was still considered overvalued, as suggested by the differential between the official and the parallel market exchange rates (about 100 percent), the deterioration in the net external position of the Bank of Ghana during the first half of 1986, and the need to maintain restrictive international payments practices to support the official exchange rate.

Floating in the Framework of an Auction Market

With a view to accelerating the adjustment of the cedi to a more appropriate level, and given the problems inherent to a fixed but adjustable exchange rate arrangement, it was decided to shift to a market arrangement for an independent float. After having established a dual exchange rate sys-

---

[8]A specific import license allowed the importer to acquire foreign exchange from the banking system, whereas a special import license carried the provision that the importer should use his own foreign exchange resources.

tem as a transitory measure, the official exchange rates were unified in the context of a "retail" auction for foreign exchange that worked fairly smoothly until its discontinuation in April 1990. This auction provided the institutional support for the achievement of an appropriate exchange rate and the gradual liberalization of Ghana's exchange and trade system.

The move toward an independently floating system in the context of an auction for foreign exchange was felt essential at this stage of Ghana's adjustment process. A further sizable depreciation of the cedi was needed to enhance Ghana's balance of payments performance, while the experience of 1985 had shown that it had become increasingly difficult to implement large discrete devaluations. The shift toward an independently floating mechanism was deemed to be one way of depoliticizing the issue of the exchange rate, as the market-determined rate would provide a more objective indication of the equilibrium exchange rate for the cedi. In addition, a floating arrangement was seen as providing for a continuous determination of the exchange rate in line with the fundamentals, whereas the previous pegged exchange rate regime had implied large discrete devaluations. Among the various possible institutional arrangements for a floating exchange rate, the authorities chose the form of the auction, as this allowed the central bank to continue to centralize the nation's foreign exchange receipts, which was viewed as crucial in minimizing capital flight. Moreover, the auction mechanism was preferred because, at least in principle, it could prevent the emergence of collusive behavior on the part of commercial banks.

To facilitate the move from a pegged regime to a floating arrangement, a transitional mechanism was designed. On September 19, 1986, a dual exchange rate system was introduced, under which one of the two windows of the arrangement was to be operated as a foreign exchange auction. The first window exchange rate was fixed at 90 cedis per U.S. dollar, while the second window exchange rate was determined by supply and demand in the new weekly auction conducted by the Bank of Ghana. Foreign exchange to cover debt service payments on official debt contracted before January 1, 1986, as well as imports of petroleum products and essential drugs, was to be provided through the first window. All other transactions, covering almost two thirds of external payments and receipts, were to be conducted through the second window. Reflecting the duality of the rates, the surrender of foreign exchange earnings to the central bank was to be effected at two different rates. Earnings from exports of cocoa and residual oil products were to be surrendered at the first window exchange rate.

Concurrently with the establishment of the new exchange rate system, a new import licensing scheme was introduced with effect from October 6, 1986. Under the new system, licenses for imports of virtually all nonconsumer goods by the private sector were to be issued without restriction. Compared with its predecessor, the new licensing system had two distinctive features. First, virtually all nonconsumer goods became eligible for foreign exchange funding from the banking system (i.e., from the auction); such access had previously been given to a more limited range of goods and only to importers who had acquired a specific import license. Second, as there were no quantitative constraints on the number of licenses, the monopoly rents that could accrue to importers under the previous system because of limitations on the number of specific import licenses were eliminated. Eligibility to bid for foreign exchange in the auction was restricted to holders of a valid import license and persons or entities having received the approval of the exchange control authorities to undertake service payments or to make an outward transfer. Traders continued to be allowed to import goods and to pay with their own foreign exchange, provided such imports were allowed under the existing Special Import License regulations.

Under the new dual exchange rate system, the Bank of Ghana auctioned foreign exchange on a weekly basis to final users of foreign exchange only; hence the "retail" nature of the auction. Authorized dealer banks had a very limited intermediary role to play in this setup, centralizing the bids for auction funds from their clients, and channeling these bids to the Bank of Ghana.

As a corollary to the selection of an auction as the institutional foundation for the market arrangement of Ghana's exchange rate system, partial surrender requirements continued to be enforced. Apart from the amount that the exporters could keep under the retention privilege scheme, all foreign exchange earnings were to be repatriated and sold to the Bank of Ghana (directly or through commercial banks). After taking into account demands for foreign exchange by the Government and by certain public entities, which were covered outside the auction but at the auction-determined rate, the Bank of Ghana decided on the amount of exchange to be auctioned. The marginal rate was used to settle all foreign exchange transactions through the second window.

One of the objectives of the auction system was to bring about a further depreciation of the cedi and to ensure a reduction in the spread between the official and parallel market exchange rates. In the event, the official exchange rate depreciated from 128 cedis per U.S. dollar at the first auction to 152 cedis per U.S. dollar at the last auction held in December 1986. This reduced the spread between the auction and the parallel market exchange rates to between 20 percent and 25 percent, compared with some 100 percent prior to the establishment of the auction. By the end of December 1986, the real effective exchange rate had depreciated by 43 percent since December 1985 and by 94 percent since March 1983.

Subsequently, the operation of the auction was modified in several ways, without however changing the retail nature of the market. Following the first auction, the system used to determine the exchange rate was changed from one in which the successful bidder pays the marginal price to a Dutch auction system, whereby successful bidders pay the bid price. More important, the two windows introduced in September 1986 were unified on February 19, 1987, in the context of the auction market, at the then prevailing rate of 150 cedis per U.S. dollar; from then on and until April 27, 1990, all transactions through the banking system were settled according to the exchange rate determined in the weekly auction.

In the framework set by the September 1986 reform, and following the unification of the two windows, access to the auction was gradually widened. First, access to the auction was widened significantly through a stepwise inclusion of additional categories of consumer goods and service payments on the list of transactions eligible for funding in the auction. As a result, the import restrictions that resulted from restricted access to foreign exchange in the auction were gradually relaxed during the 1987–89 period. The last phase of the import liberalization program was completed on February 5, 1988, when virtually all consumer goods were made eligible for funding

through the auction. As a consequence, exchange restrictions for the importation of goods into Ghana were no longer in effect and the existing administrative arrangements for import licensing became largely superfluous. Therefore, effective January 14, 1989, the import licensing system was abolished. Second, steps were taken to liberalize current invisible payments during the 1987–89 period. As a result, by the end of 1989 there remained only a few minor restrictions on payments and transfers for current international transactions, which related mainly to invisible transactions. Third, with a view to increasing the resources accruing to the auction, foreign exchange regulations were modified to curb the amount of foreign exchange being held in retention accounts. Also, the volume of cocoa exports under bilateral payments agreements that do not yield convertible foreign exchange earnings was gradually reduced to zero by late 1990.

During the January 1987–April 1990 period, the auction market functioned reasonably well. To match the increased demand resulting from the liberalization of current international transactions, the Bank of Ghana progressively increased the supply of foreign exchange to the auction (Table 5). While the weekly variation in the exchange rate of the cedi against the U.S. dollar averaged slightly more than 2 percent in 1986, the rate volatility abated in 1987, with the average weekly variation approaching 0.8 percent. Subsequently, the rate volatility continued to recede gradually, and reached 0.3 percent during the first four months of 1990. The decline in the standard deviation of weekly changes also suggests a gradually smoother pattern in exchange rate adjustments.

In addition, the efficiency of the auction market improved during 1987–90. There was a significant

Table 5. Foreign Exchange Auction: Selected Indicators, 1986–90

	1986[1]	1987	1988	1989	1990[2]	1990[3]
Average weekly supply of foreign exchange in the auction (In millions of U.S. dollars)	2.5	3.9	4.9	6.7	7.9	7.7
Average spread between highest and lowest bid rate[4]	22.5	3.9	3.7	4.4	1.1	0.8
Average spread between highest bid and marginal rate[5]	8.1	2.8	3.0	3.9	0.8	0.6
Mean weekly absolute percentage change in marginal auction rate	2.0	0.8	0.6	0.6	0.3	0.3
Standard deviation of weekly absolute percentage changes in auction rate	2.0	0.9	0.9	1.0	0.2	0.3

Sources: Bank of Ghana; and IMF staff estimates.
[1]From September 26, 1986, onward.
[2]Until April 20, 1990.
[3]From April 27, 1990, onward.
[4]In percent of the lowest bid rate.
[5]In percent of the marginal rate.

narrowing in 1987 in both the spread between the highest and the lowest bids and the difference between the highest bid and the marginal rate, as market participants became more familiar with the functioning of the auction. Subsequently, both spreads continued to decline, although each widening of the access to the auction led to a temporary increase in these spreads; this was particularly the case in early 1989.

In the event, and in line with what had been expected from the introduction of the auction, the nominal and real effective exchange rates of the cedi fell during 1987 by 40 percent and 23 percent respectively, compared with declines of 50 percent and 42 percent in 1986. Subsequently, exchange rate developments resulted in a further depreciation of the cedi of 18 percent in nominal effective terms and of 5 percent in real effective terms in 1988, and of 12 percent and 6 percent, respec-

tively, in 1989. In spite of this substantial adjustment, Ghana's exchange arrangement was still characterized by a sizable parallel market for foreign exchange that was undermining the efficiency of the official exchange rate arrangement and continued to distort the structure of economic incentives.

Absorption of Parallel Market for Foreign Exchange

In an attempt to curb the parallel market for foreign exchange and to further increase the role of market forces in determining the exchange rate, the authorities allowed, with effect from February 1, 1988, the establishment of foreign exchange bureaus (Box 2). This major institutional change proved effective to the extent that it led to the

---

Box 2. Foreign Exchange Bureaus

Under the institutional setup introduced in February 1988, foreign exchange bureaus may be operated as separate entities by any person, bank, or institution licensed by the Bank of Ghana. They are authorized to engage in the purchase and sale of foreign exchange at freely negotiated rates, each bureau being free to quote buying and selling rates. Subject to certain rules issued and enforced by the Bank of Ghana, the bureaus are not required to identify their sources of foreign exchange; similarly, sellers of foreign exchange to the bureaus are not required to identify their sources of foreign exchange. These operating rules have helped in broadening the transaction base of the exchange bureaus and have facilitated the absorption of the parallel market.

On the demand side of the new market, all bona fide import and service payments may be funded through the bureaus; in addition, capital transactions, although illegal in certain cases since capital controls continue to be applied, are a source of demand for foreign ex-

change in this market. On the supply side, the key sources are foreign exchange receipts from nontraditional exports, private remittances, and foreign exchange held by the public.

The first licensed foreign exchange bureau went into operation in April 1988; by early 1990, the number of operating bureaus had reached about 180, but several bureaus have closed down since the unification of the exchange market. The reported volume of transactions effected by the foreign exchange bureaus increased steadily from about US$1.8 million a month during the second quarter of 1988 to US$13.4 million during January–April 1990, equivalent to about 40 percent of total supply effected through the auction (Table 6).

After the unification, transactions in the bureau market expanded dramatically, reaching US$21 million a month during the last eight months of 1990, equivalent to 65 percent of the volume of transactions in the auction.

Table 6. Transactions by Foreign Exchange Bureaus, 1988–90
(In millions of U.S. dollars per month)

	1988 Second Quarter	1988 Second Semester	1989 First Semester	1989 Second Semester	1990 January–April	1990 May–December
Purchases	1.9	7.6	10.6	9.9	13.2	21.1
Sales	1.8	7.5	9.6	9.8	13.4	20.9

Sources: Bank of Ghana; and IMF staff estimates.

virtual absorption of the parallel market for foreign exchange. Moreover, while the foreign exchange bureau scheme made the structure of Ghana's official exchange arrangement temporarily more complex, it facilitated its eventual unification in early 1990. Since the inception of the foreign exchange bureau scheme, the exchange rates quoted by the bureaus have remained very close to the parallel market rate, leading to the virtual absorption of the latter in the redefined legal system.

As a result of this reform, during the April 1988–April 1990 period, Ghana maintained an exchange arrangement involving the coexistence of two spot foreign exchange markets. These two markets were segmented by the then-existing regulatory framework, as foreign exchange bureaus were not allowed to bid for foreign exchange in the weekly retail auction. This resulted in structural imbalances between supply and demand in both markets, which in turn gave rise to a persistent exchange rate differential.

Despite the improvements made in the operation of the exchange system with the introduction and the subsequent rapid development of the foreign exchange bureaus, a sizable spread persisted between the bureau and the auction rates. When the first foreign exchange bureaus became operational in April 1988, the highest selling rate was 270 cedis per U.S. dollar, close to the parallel market rate, while the highest quoted buying rate was 236 cedis per U.S. dollar. Thus, the differential between the bureau buying rate and the auction rate (expressed as a percentage of the auction rate) amounted to some 30 percent, while the spread between the auction and the bureau selling rate was about 45 percent (Chart 5). During the subsequent two years, the spread fluctuated substantially.

Beginning in March 1989, the bureau rates stabilized broadly in nominal terms vis-à-vis the U.S. dollar at their February 1989 level, while the auction rate continued to depreciate. As a result, increased convergence was achieved during 1989 and early 1990 between the foreign exchange bureau and auction rates, primarily through an increased supply of foreign exchange through the retail auction, which reduced the excess demand that had previously spilled over to the bureaus. The spread between the average bureau buying rate and the auction rate declined from a peak of about 40 percent in February 1989 to some 8 percent by late April 1990. However, more than this narrowing of the spread was needed to ensure a lasting improvement in the structure of Ghana's exchange system and economic incentives.

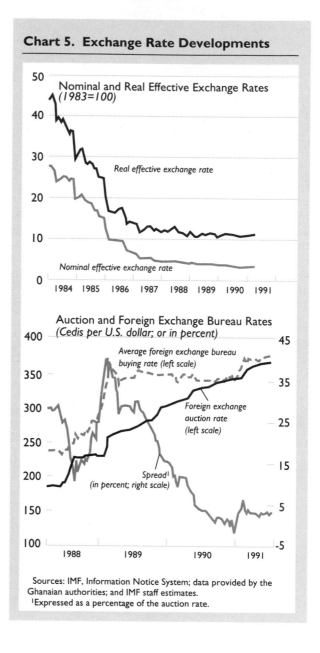

Chart 5. Exchange Rate Developments

Nominal and Real Effective Exchange Rates (1983=100)

Real effective exchange rate

Nominal effective exchange rate

Auction and Foreign Exchange Bureau Rates (Cedis per U.S. dollar; or in percent)

Average foreign exchange bureau buying rate (left scale)

Foreign exchange auction rate (left scale)

Spread[1] (in percent; right scale)

Sources: IMF, Information Notice System; data provided by the Ghanaian authorities; and IMF staff estimates.
[1]Expressed as a percentage of the auction rate.

Composite Exchange Arrangement

Regulatory and institutional changes were required to achieve the intended unification of Ghana's exchange rate arrangement. After having improved the transparency of the retail auction and enhanced the role of authorized dealers in late 1989, a wholesale auction for foreign exchange was established in late April 1990 and the retail auction was discontinued. Since then, Ghana's exchange arrangement has operated along the lines of a composite exchange rate system, combining a nascent interbank market and a wholesale auction used by the Bank of Ghana to price and distribute to authorized dealers the foreign exchange that it continues to centralize under the surrender requirements and from other sources. This has enhanced the efficiency of the exchange rate arrangement and improved the structure of economic incentives through the elimination of the price distortions stemming from the multiple currency practice inherent to the previous exchange rate arrangement. Finally, as the unification was accompanied by the completion of the liberalization of payments for current international transactions, notable progress was made toward the restoration of the financial convertibility of the cedi.

With a view to enhancing the functioning of the retail auction, the transparency of the auction was improved and some institutional changes were made in late 1989. In addition to greater publicity being given to the rules governing the retail auction for foreign exchange, new guidelines governing the auction were issued in December 1989 to enhance the intermediary role and participation of authorized dealer banks and eligible foreign exchange bureaus in the auction. Effective December 29, 1989, authorized dealer banks and eligible foreign exchange bureaus were permitted to purchase foreign exchange from the Bank of Ghana on behalf of their end-user customers. Authorized dealers were not allowed to bid on their own account, and, with the marginal exception of the bids covering the dealers' import needs, dealers' bids were to be entirely backed by firm bids by end-users of foreign exchange.

The December 1989 changes were essentially a modification of the application procedure and a decentralization of the traditional responsibilities of the Auction Secretariat that had been in charge of determining the eligibility of individual bids; from then on, eligibility was to be decided by the authorized dealer banks and eligible bureaus. In that sense, these changes were marginal amendments to the functioning of the retail auction for foreign exchange. Nevertheless, they constituted a step toward the eventual unification of Ghana's exchange rate system. They contributed to increasing the number of bidders (hence, the demand) for foreign exchange, which helped reorient the demand for foreign exchange from the bureau market toward the auction. Thereby, they proved instrumental in narrowing the spread between the bureau and the auction rates, as they helped alleviate some of the structural imbalances that were giving rise to the rate differential. In addition, they enhanced the role of authorized dealers and laid some of the foundations for the upcoming unified

arrangement in which the authorized dealers were to play a pivotal role.

Between the end of December 1989 and the end of April 1990, the higher level of transactions in the auction helped reduce the excess demand that usually spilled over to the foreign exchange bureau market. Moreover, with the further broadening of the operations of the bureaus, speculative pressure subsided as market participants became more confident about the availability of foreign exchange through the official exchange markets. As a result, the exchange rates quoted in the bureau market remained broadly stable in early 1990, while the auction rate continued to depreciate. Consequently, the spread between the bureau average buying rate and the auction rate narrowed, from an average of about 28 percent in 1989 to some 8 percent in late April 1990, facilitating the next steps toward unifying Ghana's exchange system.

On April 27, 1990, the Bank of Ghana began a wholesale foreign exchange auction and discontinued the retail auction. All authorized dealer banks were declared eligible to participate in the wholesale auction, while any licensed foreign exchange bureau could be eligible, provided it met the eligibility criteria defined on the occasion of the December 1989 amendments in the functioning of the auction. As a consequence, the foreign exchange auction and the foreign exchange bureau markets were unified.

The revised guidelines for the operation of the auction provided that authorized dealer banks and eligible foreign exchange bureaus may purchase foreign exchange from the Bank of Ghana for sale to their end-user customers and to meet their own foreign exchange needs. Accordingly, authorized dealers are now allowed to determine freely the structure of their own bids at the wholesale auction. They sell the foreign exchange obtained in the auction to their customers or to other dealers at mutually agreed rates. With a view to promoting the development of an interbank market, dealers are authorized to trade in foreign exchange among themselves or with their customers. Besides its supervisory responsibilities, the Bank of Ghana may participate as a buyer or seller in the interbank market for foreign exchange.

Under the unified exchange market, the exchange rate of the cedi is determined freely in the context of a two-tier foreign exchange market that combines the weekly price-setting in the wholesale auction with the continuous operation of the extended interbank and retail foreign exchange markets, with the exchange rates in the latter two markets superseding the auction rate for all purposes other than customs valuation and official transactions. In this composite exchange rate arrangement, a weekly auction continues to be organized by the Bank of Ghana to price[9] and distribute foreign exchange receipts centralized by the central bank under the surrender requirement scheme.[10] The partial surrender requirements were maintained on a temporary basis to give the Bank of Ghana the necessary time to strengthen its capacity for supervising the foreign exchange dealers, with a view to limiting capital flight. However, with a view to facilitating the development of a broadly based interbank market for foreign exchange, the surrender of foreign exchange earnings from exporters of goods other than cocoa and gold was shifted by the end of June 1991 from the Bank of Ghana to commercial and development banks.

Concurrently with the establishment of the wholesale auction, the remaining minor restrictions on payments for current international transactions, which related to invisible payments, were lifted. This resulted in an essentially full liberalization of Ghana's exchange system, allowing the achievement of significant progress toward the restoration of the financial convertibility of the cedi, as there were no longer any government limitations on the making of payments and transfers for current international transactions.[11] In contrast, Ghana has retained its previous controls on outward capital flows.

Since the unification on April 27, 1990, the foreign exchange market has functioned fairly smoothly. The variability of the marginal rate in the new auction remained close to the low level achieved in the retail auction before the unification. During the first two months following the reform, authorized dealer banks were rather cautious in bidding on their own account at the weekly wholesale auctions. Few transactions actually took place in the newly created interbank mar-

ket. However, authorized dealer banks became more active thereafter, trying to secure access to foreign exchange over and above the actual bid requirements of their customers and then selling the excess to the public at very small margins. While the volume of transactions in the auction remained broadly the same before and after the unification, transactions in the bureau market expanded dramatically, reaching US$21 million per month during the last eight months of 1990, equivalent to 65 percent of the volume of transactions in the auction (compared with 39 percent during the first four months of 1990).

Between the end of April 1990 and the end of December 1990, the exchange rate of the cedi in the wholesale auction depreciated by 8.7 percent vis-à-vis the U.S. dollar, reaching cedi 345 per U.S. dollar. At the same time, the cedi appreciated slightly in the foreign exchange bureau market. Consequently, the spread between the bureau and the wholesale auction rates has practically been eliminated. Moreover, the growing competition between foreign exchange bureaus resulted in a narrowing of the range within and between the buying and selling rates quoted in this market.

In summary, major progress was achieved during 1990 toward improving the structure of Ghana's exchange rate system. The market appears to have become more efficient, and the new market institutions have proven effective, making it possible to contemplate the early development of a broadly based interbank market for foreign exchange.

Policy Lessons

Ghana's experience between 1983 and 1990 shows that a gradual yet major reform of the exchange rate system, supported by judicious macroeconomic policies and the liberalization of the exchange and trade systems, fostered major progress toward correcting the initial overvaluation of the cedi and in unifying the exchange rate arrangement. The exchange reform and the exchange rate policy that it underpinned were instrumental in helping Ghana improve its macroeconomic performance. This section highlights the policy lessons that can be drawn from Ghana's experience with exchange rate policy and exchange reform.

Integrated Exchange Reform

Ghana's experience illustrates how two separate yet intrinsically related processes, namely the adjustment in the exchange rate and the process of exchange and trade reform, were carried out contiguously in a complementary manner since the

---

[9]The wholesale auction system continues to be conducted on the basis of the Dutch pricing system.

[10]Under these surrender requirements, most exporters are required to collect and repatriate in full the proceeds from their exports within 60 days of shipment. Exporters are generally allowed to retain up to 35 percent of their export proceeds in foreign exchange accounts with the domestic banking system for financing essential imports.

[11]The concept of currency convertibility has a number of meanings. The concept used here refers to the notion of convertibility fostered by the IMF referring to the unrestricted and nondiscriminatory right of the residents of member countries to use domestic currency to effect payments and transfers for current international transactions. More precisely, the IMF's concept of financial convertibility, as defined in its Articles of Agreement (Article VIII) refers to the absence of government limitations on the making of payments and transfers. For an analysis of the concept of currency convertibility, see Gilman (1990).

inception of the economic recovery program. Within the overall macroeconomic strategy adopted in 1983, a central role was assigned to exchange rate policy, notably with a view to attaining the balance of payments objectives. It was decided not to use the official exchange rate as a nominal anchor for the domestic price level; instead, credit and incomes policies were to play that role in the context of the adjustment program. This policy choice reflected the fact that the balance of payments constraint was seen as the overriding problem, owing to the prevailing scarcity of foreign exchange. In addition, it was considered that the inflationary impulse associated with a devaluation of the official exchange rate would be limited, since most of the transactions were conducted at the prevailing parallel exchange rate. Finally, a decisive exchange rate action was warranted; if this instrument had been excluded from the menu of policy options, a prolonged period of fiscal and monetary contraction would have been required given the severity of the initial external imbalances and the steep loss of international competitiveness. An adjustment strategy devoid of the exchange rate instrument would have involved considerable output losses and, therefore, might have been difficult to sustain.

The magnitude of the initial devaluations contrasts with the gradualism that characterized the reform of the institutional setup of the exchange arrangement. In fact, after the inception of the economic recovery program and the first exchange rate actions, seven years elapsed before Ghana reached an appropriate market-determined exchange rate in the context of a liberalized system for current international transactions and a fully unified exchange rate system. This gradualist approach to adopting a floating system in a unified setting had two main purposes.

On the one hand, given the magnitude of the initial overvaluation of the cedi, gradualism in the structural reform process made the transition to a unified and floating system easier than it might otherwise have been, particularly from a political and social point of view. The adjustment reform path that was chosen allowed the authorities to overcome the reservations initially expressed regarding the risks of floating the cedi in the early stages of the economic recovery program. These risks included the potential loss of control over the exchange rate, which could have degenerated into an inflation/depreciation spiral, the intensification of capital flight, and the destabilization of Ghana's productive system. The latter was a particular concern, as the period preceding the program had been marked by a severe dislocation of Ghana's productive system. In view of these distortions, it

was feared that floating the rate would involve an overshooting of the equilibrium rate and would not yield a sufficient supply response in the short and medium term. In that regard, gradualism in the reform process was perceived by the authorities as helping to limit the transitional costs in terms of output losses and associated unemployment by allowing the required transfer of resources across sectors of the economy to be stretched over a longer period.

On the other hand, the macroeconomic imbalances that initially plagued the economy were such that a strong fiscal adjustment was seen as an absolute requisite for a successful exchange rate adjustment, especially as policy credibility was low during the first phase of the reforms. Accordingly, it was accepted that the pace of exchange reform would be set in part by the feasible fiscal and monetary adjustments. Hence, the choice was made not to float the cedi at the outset of the program, but instead to wait until the public finances had been brought under control and more foreign exchange resources were available to sustain a floating rate system. Meanwhile, the exchange rate was depreciated through a series of large discrete devaluations.

A central feature of Ghana's adjustment strategy is that the exchange rate actions were in general accompanied and supported by a tightening of demand-management policies, notably through a reduction of fiscal deficits. Fiscal policy aimed at restoring fiscal discipline at an early stage while the tax system was reformed to boost revenue and strengthen economic incentives. Major progress was made during the first phase of the economic recovery program in achieving fiscal consolidation (see Section IV).

In contrast, monetary policy did not prove fully supportive of the exchange rate policy; in spite of a marked slowdown in the rate of growth of the net domestic assets of the banking system, especially during 1985–89, the rate of monetary expansion remained high and interest rates did not reach satisfactory levels in real terms. This contributed to the continued downward adjustment in the nominal exchange rate beyond what was needed to correct the initial overvaluation and to match both the deterioration in the external terms of trade and the liberalization of current international transactions.

Admittedly, it is difficult to establish unequivocally whether the reform strategy adopted since 1983 constituted, in Ghana's context, the 'best route' toward full unification, but the experience certainly shows that the path that was chosen delivered the intended result without major disruptions, although this came about only at the end of an extended transitory period.[12] In any event, Ghana's experience shows the feasibility, although not necessarily the optimality, of a gradualist approach to correcting major overvaluations and unifying exchange rate systems, provided the various steps adopted throughout the process are decisive enough and supported by appropriate macroeconomic and structural policies.[13]

Ghana's exchange rate reform took place in the context of a gradual yet far-reaching program of exchange and trade liberalization. The import licensing system was first streamlined, then liberalized, and finally abolished in early 1989, while other current transactions were progressively made eligible for funding through the auction. By late April 1990, Ghana's exchange and trade system was basically free of restrictions on payments and transfers for current international transactions. This reform included two important features that greatly facilitated the absorption of the parallel markets into the legal economic channels, namely the early legalization of imports financed by foreign exchange acquired in the parallel market under the Special Import License scheme, and the legalization of the parallel market for foreign exchange through the foreign exchange bureau scheme. Moreover, the redirection of incentives and resources that was to result from the adjustment in the exchange rate was supported by a dismantling of a previously extensive system of price controls. This allowed a broad pass-through of higher import costs to domestic wholesale and retail prices, including those of petroleum products.

Finally, since 1983, Ghana's economic policies under the economic recovery program have been supported by the international community. The increase in foreign financial inflows was a prerequisite for the reconstruction of Ghana's economic infrastructure and the rehabilitation of the potentially viable parts of the country's productive system. In addition, the significant increase in external financial resources helped sustain both the

floating of the exchange rate and the liberalization of the current international transactions, limiting the magnitude of the required adjustment in the real effective exchange rate. This also allowed the gradual reduction in outstanding external payments arrears, the eventual clearance of which was achieved in June 1990.

Flexible Exchange Rate Policy

The exchange rate strategy followed since 1983 has contributed to a notable recovery in Ghana's exports and output, helped the country cope with a severe deterioration in its external terms of trade since 1986, and facilitated the liberalization of Ghana's exchange and trade regime. Together with the virtually full liberalization of payments and transfers for current international transactions, the exchange rate policy and exchange reform have restored the profitability of investment in traded goods sectors, thus providing the appropriate signals for a reallocation of resources toward sectors in which Ghana has a strong comparative advantage such as cocoa, gold, timber, and various agro-industries. As early as 1984, the adjustment in the exchange rate allowed a significant increase in cocoa producer prices, without adverse implications for the budget. Improved price incentives led to a rapid recovery in cocoa output and to a gradual decline in the share of cocoa beans that were exported through illegal channels to neighboring countries. Both supply responses were crucial elements of a strategy aimed at attaining balance of payments viability over the medium term. More generally, the export volume of all Ghana's major export items, including gold and timber, has increased substantially since 1983. As a result, Ghana's export performance has been impressive; over the 1984–90 period, Ghana's export volume grew by more than 94 percent while that of the whole sub-Saharan African region increased by only 21 percent. Meanwhile, Ghana's export base has been diversified. After an initial deterioration as cocoa led the recovery in exports during 1983–86, the aggregate index of concentration of Ghana's export base declined (i.e., improved), essentially as a result of developments in the primary goods sector (Table 7).

Admittedly, the importance of manufacturing as a foreign exchange earner remained marginal; while the supply response of nontraditional exports to the strengthened incentives has been fairly strong, the base was very low. Nevertheless, the shift in the pattern of production and the associated broadening of the export base have reduced the vulnerability of the economy to external shocks. They have already helped dampen the

---

[12]In that regard, Pinto (1988b) argues that "if policy credibility is low and initial level of the premium high, with significant revenue and redistributive implications, the pace of reform should be set by the feasible speed of fiscal reform. . . . The 'best route' consequently might be to gradually relax rationing, accompanying this with discrete devaluation, with the pace of reform being set by the speed of fiscal reform." See also Pinto (1988a) for similar conclusions.

[13]Reviewing the experience of nine African countries that introduced floating exchange rate regimes in the 1980s, Kimaro (1988) also underlined the crucial importance of early and sustained decisive fiscal adjustments, as well as the timely disbursement of balance of payments support, to the success of the newly introduced floats.

Table 7. Gini-Hirschman Index of Concentration of the Export Base, 1983–90[1]

	1983	1984	1985	1986	1987	1988	1989	1990
At current prices	67	70	67	69	64	58	56	55
At constant prices	67	63	58	55	52	52	56	56

Source: IMF staff estimates.

[1]The Gini-Hirschman concentration index is used here to measure the degree of diversification of the export base. The higher the value of the index (i.e., the closer it is to 100), the more concentrated the country's export base.

variability in export earnings since 1987, given the low covariance of the export prices of cocoa, timber, gold, and nontraditional export items. Moreover, the flexible exchange rate policy pursued in recent years has helped cushion the impact on the economy of the sharp deterioration in the terms of trade experienced since 1986.[14]

The restored profitability of export and import-substituting industries helped alleviate the initial foreign exchange crisis that had severely impeded growth and development. The increased availability of foreign exchange has facilitated a substantial increase in imports, which was essential to the rehabilitation of Ghana's productive base. During the 1984–90 period, Ghana's import volume increased by some 100 percent on a cumulative basis, while that of the whole sub-Saharan African region virtually stagnated.

Furthermore, the exchange rate adjustment has been instrumental in bringing about a redistribution of income between urban and rural areas to the benefit of the latter. This has been achieved in large part through a more appropriate producer price policy in the cocoa sector that has bolstered incentives for cocoa farmers. More generally, the liberalization of the exchange and trade regime has eliminated a number of rent-seeking activities that were related to the previous policy environment.

Moreover, Ghana's experience suggests that at least in certain circumstances, exchange rate depreciations may facilitate fiscal adjustment. In fact, the Ghanaian authorities intentionally used devaluations to raise government revenue during 1983–86. Since taxes on international trade had previously provided a significant part of government revenue, whereas foreign exchange expenditure had represented a smaller share of total government expenditure, the depreciations of the exchange rate had a direct positive effect on the

budget. Similarly, they had the mechanical impact of boosting the cedi value of the growing disbursements of external official grants. At times, between 1983 and 1986, the authorities even appeared to focus more on the need to increase revenue and on achieving their fiscal targets rather than on competitiveness considerations in deciding the magnitude and/or the frequency of exchange rate adjustments.[15]

Fiscal adjustment contributed to the steady deceleration of growth in net domestic assets and of inflation. Despite the magnitude of the adjustments in the exchange rate, inflation declined appreciably during the 1983–89 period. While it is likely that the substantial adjustments in the exchange rate had a significant impact on the domestic currency cost of tradable goods, it would appear that the pass-through coefficient of the depreciation of the official exchange rate was quite low, particularly during the early phases of the economic recovery program. As most imported goods were available only at prices that reflected the parallel exchange market rate, the response of the tradable goods prices was not commensurate with the change in the official external value of the cedi. This would suggest that at least until a significant share of consumer goods imports became eligible for funding through the auction, the parallel market exchange rate was the relevant cost-push variable. However, it appears that during the last few years, in a context in which most imports have been financed through the auction, the continued depreciation of the auction rate has contributed to the pick-up in inflation through cost-push effects (see Section VI). In any event, the correction of the massive overvaluation that prevailed prior to 1983 and the subsequent unifica-

---

[14]Ghana's external terms of trade are estimated to have deteriorated by about 37 percent on a cumulative basis during 1987–90. On an end-of-period basis, the real effective exchange rate of the cedi depreciated by 36 percent between August 1986 and December 1990.

[15]According to J.S. Addo, former Governor of the Bank of Ghana, "under the programme, . . . the flexible exchange rate policy was [inter alia] to reinforce the tax base since external trade provided the bulk of government revenue. Under the new system, budget performance was reviewed frequently (at quarterly intervals) and, depending on the size of the deficit, the exchange rate was determined." (See Addo (1990).)

tion have not led to an uncontrollable inflationary spiral as supportive fiscal and credit policies were implemented in a timely fashion.

Concluding Remarks

In sum, since 1983, the implementation of a flexible exchange rate policy and the progressive liberalization of the exchange and trade system have been key elements of Ghana's adjustment policies. Moreover, Ghana's experience exemplifies a strategy that blends a series of decisive devaluations with a gradual reform of the exchange and trade system. These policy changes allowed a substantial increase in the efficiency of the exchange system, as progress was made toward a unified exchange rate system and currency convertibility. The resulting improvement in the structure of economic incentives helped Ghana strengthen its external and growth performance as well as absorb parallel markets while an acceleration of inflation was avoided, in large part because more appropriate fiscal and credit policies were implemented.

V Fiscal Adjustment

Fiscal policies since 1983 have been an integral part of Ghana's overall economic strategy of financial and structural adjustment. These policies have been focused on lowering the imbalances in government finances, thus easing the task of monetary policy and contributing to a reduction in the external current account deficit. In addition, fiscal policies have been directed at fostering economic growth through a rehabilitation and expansion of the productive capacity of the economy and a strengthening of economic incentives through tax reforms, while promoting a more equitable distribution of income and the benefits from adjustment.

This section begins with a description of the deterioration in Ghana's fiscal position up to 1983, followed by a review of the Government's policy response. The resulting trends in the fiscal deficit, government savings, and the levels and composition of government revenue and expenditure are examined and evaluated, with particular emphasis on their implications for income distribution.

Fiscal Deterioration Prior to 1983

During the years prior to 1983, inappropriate domestic policies and exogenous shocks resulted in a protracted economic decline, as well as a dramatic deterioration in the public finances of Ghana. Large fiscal deficits, financed by borrowing from the domestic banking system, had led to an acceleration in inflation and an increasingly overvalued exchange rate. Pervasive government intervention in the economy—through extensive price, distribution, and import controls, as well as a massive expansion of the role of public enterprises—had severely distorted economic incentives. These developments had induced a shift of economic activity to informal markets and encouraged the expansion of unrecorded cross-border trade, thereby causing a sharp contraction in the tax base and, consequently, in the ability of the Government to mobilize resources.

By 1983, Ghana's tax revenue had declined to just 4.6 percent of GDP and total revenue to 5.6 percent of GDP—about one third of its 1970 level—compared with more than 21 percent for Africa as a whole, and over 14 percent for sub-Saharan Africa (Table 8). As a result of the decline in revenue, government expenditure had been cut sharply, services had declined, and the economic and social infrastructure of Ghana had deteriorated. Capital spending, for instance, plummeted from 4.5 percent of GDP in 1975 to only 0.6 percent of GDP by 1983 (Table 9); spending on health, education, social security, and welfare fell, over the same period, from 8.7 percent of GDP to 2.3 percent. In addition to a shortage of material inputs, there was an exodus of qualified personnel from the civil service in response to a compression of real public sector wages; between 1975 and 1983, public sector wages rose at an annual rate of approximately 35 percent, while prices increased at an average rate of 73 percent. At the same time, attempts to increase tax revenue without altering the structure of the tax system led to high marginal tax rates on a shrinking base. The result was a further deterioration in economic incentives and an accelerated shift of economic activity to the underground economy.

Policy Response

Ghana's fiscal policy since 1983 has been aimed at correcting the fiscal imbalances, reforming the tax system to augment revenue collection and to enhance economic incentives, increasing public and private savings, and rehabilitating the economic and social infrastructure. Broadly, the process of fiscal adjustment has been a success. Both revenue and expenditure have risen markedly as a proportion of GDP over the period, and the fiscal deficit has declined (Chart 6). In addition, capital expenditure has increased as a share of total spending, government savings have risen, and greater attention has been paid to the provision of

Table 8. Central Government Revenue and Grants, 1975–91

	1975	1980	1983	1984	1985	1986	1987	1988	1989	1990	1991 Budget
						(In percent of total revenue and grants)					
Tax revenue	89.8	90.6	82.6	79.2	80.7	84.5	85.5	84.0	81.4	82.2	84.4
Direct taxes	20.6	26.0	18.0	18.2	19.2	19.2	21.7	26.3	21.4	20.6	16.9
Individual	8.5	11.8	8.6	7.3	7.6	7.2	7.4	7.2	5.7	6.5	5.2
Corporate	11.3	14.2	8.8	10.6	10.8	11.3	13.0	18.0	14.6	12.7	10.8
Other	0.8	0.1	0.6	0.3	0.7	0.7	1.4	1.1	1.0	1.4	1.0
Taxes on domestic goods and services	16.7	47.3	15.9	24.6	22.3	26.6	23.6	25.2	24.3	26.8	36.9
General sales	5.7	6.7	2.3	1.9	2.9	4.3	7.5	8.0	8.3	8.8	7.3
Excise except petroleum	10.5	41.1	13.6	22.6	17.9	13.4	11.5	9.7	8.9	8.6	7.9
Petroleum	—	—	—	—	1.5	9.0	4.5	7.4	7.0	9.5	21.7
Taxes on international trade and transactions	52.5	17.1	48.7	36.4	39.3	38.7	40.2	32.5	35.7	34.7	30.6
Import duties	17.2	16.3	19.3	14.0	16.3	19.3	16.0	16.6	21.0	24.6	20.2
Export duties	35.3	0.8	28.6	22.0	22.8	19.3	24.2	15.9	14.6	10.2	10.3
Non-tax revenue	10.1	8.0	16.9	16.8	15.3	10.3	9.1	8.5	8.7	7.4	6.8
Grants	0.1	1.4	0.6	4.0	4.0	5.3	5.4	7.5	9.9	10.4	8.7
						(In percent of GDP)					
Tax revenue	13.8	7.4	4.6	6.6	9.5	12.2	12.7	12.3	12.3	11.6	13.8
Direct taxes	3.2	2.1	1.0	1.5	2.3	2.8	3.2	3.9	3.2	2.9	2.8
Taxes on domestic goods and services	2.6	3.8	0.9	2.1	2.6	3.8	3.5	3.7	3.7	3.8	6.0
Taxes on international trade and transactions	8.1	1.4	2.7	3.0	4.6	5.6	6.0	4.8	5.4	4.9	5.0
Non-tax revenue	1.6	0.6	0.9	1.4	1.8	1.5	1.4	1.2	1.3	1.0	1.1
Grants	—	0.1	—	0.3	0.5	0.8	0.8	1.1	1.5	1.5	1.4
Total revenue and grants	15.4	8.1	5.6	8.4	11.7	14.4	14.9	14.6	15.1	14.1	16.3
Memorandum items											
Total revenue and grants (broad)	—	—	5.6	8.8	12.4	15.9	16.7	16.1	16.8	15.8	18.1
Grants (broad)	—	—	—	0.7	1.1	2.2	2.6	2.5	3.2	3.2	3.2

Sources: Data provided by the Ghanaian authorities; and IMF staff estimates.

social services. Finally, tax reforms over this period have altered the composition of tax revenue and have strengthened incentives to produce, save, and invest.

Fiscal reform under the economic recovery program can be broadly divided into three overlapping stages. In the initial stage, 1983–84, the Government responded to the fiscal deterioration by relying on expenditure cuts and the restoration of the tax base to generate increased revenue. In the second stage, covering 1985–86, the objectives of fiscal policy were broadened to include, besides fiscal stabilization, the rehabilitation and expansion of the basic economic and social infrastructure. Finally, in the third stage, beginning in 1987, increased emphasis was attached to further strengthening economic incentives, particularly for private savings and investment, and promoting equity. These three stages of fiscal adjustment do not represent distinct and unrelated sets of policies; rather they simply delineate periods in which one or another set of objectives was given particular emphasis.

First Stage: Restoring Fiscal Balance

One of the priorities of the economic recovery program was to restore discipline in government finances. To this end, in 1983, the first year of implementation of the adjustment strategy, the budget deficit was reduced from 6.3 percent of GDP in 1982 to 2.7 percent of GDP, primarily through a contraction in government spending, from 10.2 percent of GDP to 8.0 percent. This lower spending level was significantly below the budgeted level of 9.5 percent of GDP and was necessitated by a shortfall in government revenue.

Table 9. Central Government Expenditure and Net Lending, 1975–91

	1975	1980	1983	1984	1985	1986	1987	1988	1989	1990	1991 Budget
				Economic Classification							
				(In percent of total expenditure and net lending)							
Total expenditure	94.6	96.7	97.2	97.1	95.6	96.4	95.5	96.0	96.2	96.4	96.9
Current expenditure	75.1	82.2	89.4	84.9	80.3	83.0	75.3	74.1	72.8	75.1	74.7
Goods and services	50.2	48.4	47.9	56.9	57.4	57.5	56.5	56.7	54.8	54.5	54.2
Wages and salaries	30.1	28.5	24.7	19.2	30.3	35.7	33.6	33.0	30.8	31.2	30.4
Other goods and services	20.1	19.9	23.2	37.7	27.0	21.7	22.9	23.7	24.0	23.4	23.8
Interest payments	6.1	12.8	14.5	12.5	10.6	15.5	9.9	8.0	9.2	10.3	10.7
Subsidies and transfers	13.7	21.0	27.0	15.5	12.3	10.0	9.0	9.4	8.8	10.2	9.8
Capital expenditure	19.5	14.4	7.9	12.3	15.2	13.4	17.3	19.9	18.7	18.3	19.0
Special efficiency	—	—	—	—	—	—	2.8	2.0	4.7	3.0	3.2
Net lending	5.4	3.3	2.8	2.9	4.4	3.6	4.5	4.0	3.8	3.6	3.1
				(In percent of GDP)							
Total expenditure	21.7	19.1	8.0	9.9	13.3	13.8	13.7	13.7	13.9	13.5	14.0
Current expenditure	17.2	16.3	7.4	8.6	11.2	11.9	10.8	10.6	10.5	10.5	10.8
Capital expenditure	4.5	2.9	0.6	1.2	2.1	1.9	2.5	2.8	2.7	2.5	2.8
Total expenditure and net lending	22.9	20.0	8.2	10.2	14.0	14.3	14.3	14.3	14.4	14.0	14.5
Memorandum items											
Capital expenditure (broad)	—	—	0.6	1.9	3.3	5.0	5.4	5.8	5.1	5.0	5.9
Total expenditure (broad)	—	—	8.2	11.1	15.4	19.2	19.1	18.9	18.9	18.1	19.3
				Functional Classification							
				(In percent of total central government expenditure)							
General public services	25.8	21.0	26.4	24.9	21.3	20.8	19.3	22.0	19.3	...	...
Defense	7.8	6.3	4.6	6.0	7.5	6.5	6.5	3.2	3.1	...	...
Education	20.6	17.1	20.4	20.2	18.0	23.9	23.9	25.7	24.3	...	...
Health	8.3	6.4	4.4	8.6	9.8	8.3	8.3	9.0	10.1	...	...
Social security and welfare	11.0	7.2	4.3	4.2	5.0	5.3	6.4	6.9	7.3	...	...
Housing and community amenities	—	—	1.7	2.1	2.0	1.9	1.9	3.5	2.6	...	...
Other community and social services	3.9	3.1	1.8	2.2	1.5	1.7	1.7	1.5	2.0	...	...
Economic services[2]	16.2	22.7	21.6	18.9	23.8	15.4	18.6	17.9	16.9	...	...
Interest on public debt	6.5	13.2	14.9	12.8	11.1	16.1	10.4	8.3	9.5	...	...
Special efficiency	—	—	—	—	—	—	2.9	2.1	4.9	...	...

Sources: Data provided by the Ghanaian authorities; and IMF staff estimates.
[1]Data for 1975 and 1980 are on a fiscal year basis (year ending March); from 1983 onward the fiscal year coincides with the calender year.
[2]Includes services for agriculture, forestry and fishing, mining, manufacturing and construction, roads, and other transport and communication.

Thus, domestic borrowing was reduced to 2.3 percent of GDP, from 4.3 percent the previous year. Foreign financing began to recover, as the stabilization efforts of the authorities led to renewed donor interest.

The 1984 budget benefited from the impact of exchange rate adjustments on receipts from cocoa taxes and import duties; the increased availability of foreign exchange earnings was expected to facilitate an expansion in imports. Discretionary tax policy changes were, in fact, largely aimed at lowering the tax burden; for instance, the lowest income tax bracket was raised and the marginal tax rates lowered to reduce the average effective rate of personal income tax. In the event, while the level of imports, and thus of import duties, was lower than expected, the revenue/GDP ratio did rise in 1984 to 8.4 percent of GDP from 5.6 percent of GDP in 1983, while the deficit declined further to 1.8 percent of GDP (Table 10).[16]

---

[16]The budget deficit is calculated on a narrow basis. It excludes expenditure financed by external project grants and loans, but includes program grants as revenue. See below for a discussion of alternative measures of the budget deficit.

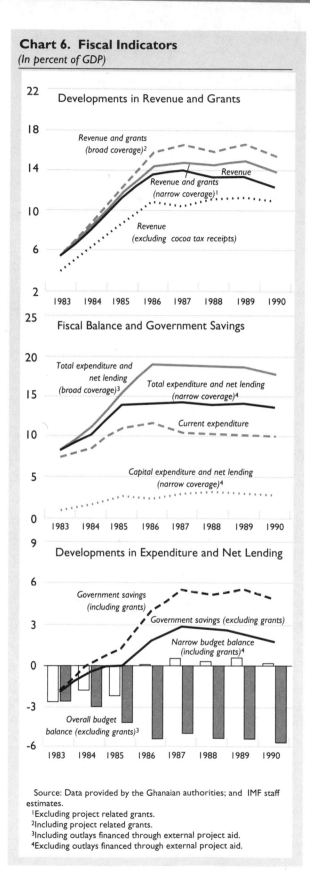

Chart 6. Fiscal Indicators
(In percent of GDP)

Developments in Revenue and Grants

Revenue and grants (broad coverage)[2]

Revenue

Revenue and grants (narrow coverage)[1]

Revenue (excluding cocoa tax receipts)

Fiscal Balance and Government Savings

Total expenditure and net lending (broad coverage)[3]

Total expenditure and net lending (narrow coverage)[4]

Current expenditure

Capital expenditure and net lending (narrow coverage)[4]

Developments in Expenditure and Net Lending

Government savings (including grants)

Government savings (excluding grants)

Narrow budget balance (including grants)[4]

Overall budget balance (excluding grants)[3]

Source: Data provided by the Ghanaian authorities; and IMF staff estimates.
[1] Excluding project related grants.
[2] Including project related grants.
[3] Including outlays financed through external project aid.
[4] Excluding outlays financed through external project aid.

Second Stage: Rehabilitating the Economic Infrastructure

The 1985 budget incorporated a more growth-oriented fiscal strategy. Government capital spending was expanded in the context, from 1986 onward, of a rolling three-year public investment program, thus necessitating a stepped-up mobilization of domestic revenue. Exchange rate adjustments in 1985 contributed to higher revenue from taxes on international trade, while the general economic recovery resulted in a higher collection of taxes on domestic goods and services and on corporate incomes. Total expenditure and net lending rose from 10.2 percent of GDP in 1984 to 14.0 percent in 1985, led by jumps in capital expenditure and outlays on wages and salaries; capital spending increased from 1.2 percent of GDP to 2.1 percent, while the wage bill was raised from the equivalent of 2.0 percent of GDP to 4.2 percent. In 1986, a similarly large expansion in government spending was planned, but shortfalls in revenue relative to the budget estimates necessitated a tighter control over expenditure; in the event, total spending rose only marginally, to 14.3 percent of GDP. Capital spending declined slightly, to 1.9 percent of GDP, but the wage bill continued to increase, reaching 5.1 percent of GDP.

With a view to encouraging private investment, an Investment Code was introduced in 1985, providing a broad range of tax incentives to domestic and foreign investors. These incentives—such as exemption from import duties, lower corporate tax rates, and accelerated depreciation allowances—varied widely by industry and activity. The specificity of these incentives, however, made the taxsblaw inefficient and somewhat difficult to administer.

Third Stage: Fiscal Policy, Efficiency, and Equity

Since 1987, the focus of fiscal policy has been broadened to encompass enhancing the efficiency and equity of the tax system. Revenue and expenditure have remained more or less flat as a share of GDP for most of this period, but the pace of tax reform has accelerated, and more attention is being paid to strengthening private sector incentives. In addition, more care has been taken to cushion the impact of both tax and expenditure policies on the most vulnerable members of the society. Tax administration has also been strengthened through efforts to increase tax compliance among the self-employed and to monitor more closely corporate accounts, while efforts have been made to im-

Table 10. Measures of Central Government Fiscal Deficit, Financing, and Government Savings, 1975–91

(In percent of GDP)

	1975	1980	1983	1984	1985	1986	1987	1988	1989	1990	1991 Budget
Narrow surplus or deficit[1]											
Including grants	−7.6	−11.0	−2.7	−1.8	−2.2	0.1	0.5	0.4	0.7	0.2	1.9
Excluding grants	−7.6	−11.1	−2.7	−2.1	−2.7	−0.7	−0.3	−0.7	−0.8	−1.3	0.4
Broad surplus or deficit											
Including grants	—	—	−2.7	−2.3	−3.0	−3.3	−2.4	−2.8	−2.1	−2.4	−1.2
Excluding grants	—	—	−2.7	−3.1	−4.1	−5.5	−5.1	−5.3	−5.3	−5.5	−4.4
Financing (of narrow balance)	7.6	11.0	2.7	1.8	2.2	−0.1	−0.5	−0.4	−0.7	−0.2	−1.9
Foreign (net)	—	0.9	0.4	0.7	1.0	−1.1	−0.2	0.2	0.3	1.3	0.9
Borrowing	—	—	1.1	1.9	2.8	2.6	3.2	4.0	3.8	3.0	2.2
Repayments	—	—	−0.7	−1.2	−1.8	−3.7	−3.3	−3.8	−3.5	−1.8	−1.2
Domestic (net)	7.6	10.1	2.3	1.1	1.2	1.0	−0.4	−0.6	−1.1	−1.4	−2.8
Of which: Banking system	7.0	3.8	1.4	1.1	0.9	0.5	−1.0	−0.9	−1.0	−1.1	−2.1
Government savings[2]											
Narrow basis											
Including grants	−1.9	−8.1	−1.8	−0.3	0.5	2.5	3.7	3.8	4.0	3.2	5.1
Excluding grants	−1.9	−8.3	−1.8	−0.6	0.1	1.7	2.9	2.7	2.5	1.8	3.6
Broad basis											
Including grants	—	—	−1.8	0.1	1.1	4.0	5.5	5.2	5.7	4.9	6.8
Excluding grants	—	—	−1.8	−0.6	0.1	1.7	2.9	2.7	2.5	1.8	3.6

Sources: Data provided by the Ghanaian authorities; and IMF staff estimates.

[1]Negative numbers indicate a deficit. Budget coverage excludes capital expenditure financed through external project aid, as well as the corresponding grants and loans.

[2]Calculated as the difference between total revenue and current expenditure, including special efficiency.

prove the efficiency of government financial operations.

On the direct tax side, corporate tax rates were lowered in 1988 from 55 percent to 45 percent for businesses in manufacturing, farming, and exporting, and from 55 percent to 50 percent in 1989 for the remaining firms, other than those in banking, insurance, commercial activities, and printing. The 1991 budget provided for a further reduction to 35 percent in the corporate tax rate applicable to agriculture, manufacturing, real estate, construction, and services and extended to all enterprises in the manufacturing sector capital allowances provided under the Investment Code. These measures were complemented by a sharp reduction in the capital gains tax rate to 5 percent, with income from mergers and acquisitions and publicly traded shares exempted from capital gains tax, and a reduction in the withholding tax on dividends from 30 percent to 15 percent. These tax reforms created an environment more conducive for private savings and investment.

The personal income tax burden was also lowered during 1987–89 through substantial upward adjustments in personal allowances and tax brackets, thus reducing the average effective income tax rate. The 1991 budget provided for further increases in personal allowances and tax brackets, at rates well in excess of expected inflation. In addition, the personal income tax base was broadened to include, after July 1991, all allowances paid to employees in both the public and private sectors;[17] to offset the impact of this measure on disposable incomes, the top marginal rate of personal income taxation was lowered from 55 percent to 25 percent.

Receipts from import duties expanded during 1987–90, with their share in total revenue rising from 16 percent to nearly 25 percent (Table 8), as a result of a major increase in the domestic

---

[17]Comprising mainly allowances for housing, transport, leave, and meals.

currency value of imports, stemming from the depreciation of the exchange rate of the cedi and sharp increases in the volume of imports, as well as improved tax administration. The gradual removal of import licensing requirements has also encouraged imports of consumer goods, thus contributing to the broadening of the import tax base.[18] Duty rates were lowered by an additional 5 percentage points in 1988; at present, the primary import tariff rate applied to most goods is 25 percent, but special import taxes raise nominal protection for some products up to 60 percent.

At the same time, export duties (since 1987, levied exclusively on cocoa) have declined, as a percentage of total revenue, from 28.6 percent in 1983 to 10.2 percent in 1990, with most of that reduction taking place since 1987. The cocoa levy is determined as a 100 percent duty on all proceeds from cocoa exports, net of payments to cocoa farmers and the marketing and other operational costs of the Cocoa Board.[19] The decline in the receipts from the cocoa tax as a share of total revenue reflects the weakening in world cocoa prices as well as the substantial real increases in the producer price paid to cocoa farmers, consistent with the Government's goal of increasing incentives to produce and export cocoa. The cocoa farmers' share in the f.o.b. cocoa export price has risen dramatically, from 9 percent for the 1984/85 crop year to 47 percent for 1990/91. The losses from the cocoa tax since 1987, as a percentage of GDP, more than offset gains from other taxes, resulting in a decline in the tax/GDP ratio during 1988–90.

The system of indirect taxation has also been reformed in the last several years; in 1987, all excise duties on products other than petroleum, beverages, and tobacco were abolished, with the revenue loss compensated for by an increase in the standard general sales tax rate from 10 to 20 percent and subsequently to 25 percent; in 1989, this rate was reduced to 22.5 percent and in the context of the 1991 budget was lowered further to 17.5 percent. Meanwhile, the windfall profit on petroleum, transferred to the budget in 1986, was converted to a specific excise duty on petroleum products in 1987, ensuring that revenue would accrue to the budget even in the event of a rise in world oil prices. The following year, petroleum tax rates were more than doubled and have since been raised markedly, including an increase from 5 cedis per liter (about 10 percent of the retail price)

to 65 cedis per liter in 1990 (about 35 percent of the current average retail price). As a result, the importance of petroleum taxes is expected to grow sharply in 1991, with receipts projected to constitute 22 percent of all revenue and to virtually triple as a ratio to GDP, to 3.5 percent.

On the expenditure side, the Government's main objectives have been (a) to raise civil service wages to more competitive levels, as well as widen the differential between the highest- and lowest-paid civil servants, in order to attract and retain highly skilled staff; (b) to channel additional resources to capital expenditure for the rehabilitation of the nation's infrastructure, with appropriate allocations for outlays on operations and maintenance, particularly in the priority sectors of agriculture, education, and health; and (c) to ensure that the benefits of economic reforms are broadly shared and that problems of poverty are addressed. Notwithstanding the overall budgetary constraints, progress has been made in all these areas since 1986.

The differential between the highest- and lowest-paid civil servants was raised from 5.4 to 1 in 1988 to 9.4 to 1 in 1990. However, the budgeted general increases in real wage rates have, in recent years, been eroded by higher-than-expected inflation. For instance, the increase in the Government's wage bill in 1990 deflated by the targeted rate of inflation—a measure of the expected real wage increase at the time of the budget—was nearly 6 percent, while wages deflated by actual inflation declined by almost 5 percent. In the 1991 budget, the wage bill is projected to increase by approximately 26 percent, allowing both an across-the-board wage increase of 27 percent compared with wage levels in early 1990, as well as an additional stretching of relative wages between the highest- and lowest-paid employees to 10.5 to 1.

The objective of increasing real wages and broadening wage differentials in the civil service has been pursued within the context of a policy of civil service reform, which aimed in addition at reducing overstaffing and restructuring pay and grading management to establish a better basis for a performance-oriented civil service. Under this program, some 50,000 mainly unskilled civil servants were redeployed during 1987–90, although owing to the hiring of needed skilled staff, the net reduction amounted to approximately 30,000.[20] A further net redeployment of some 5,000 workers is planned for 1991. As part of the effort to share the benefits of adjustment, a "special efficiency bud-

---

[18]Nonetheless, the import tax base is still fairly narrow, as it excludes aid-related imports, private imports under the Capital Investment Act, and imports by certain state enterprises.

[19]Income from cocoa farming, both for individuals and companies, is exempt from direct taxation.

---

[20]This amounts to about 10 percent of the civil service, which includes the military and other security employees, as well as the education service.

get" was established in 1987 to cover the costs of retraining and supporting redeployed public sector employees.

Ghana's public investment program has been aiming at the rehabilitation and expansion of the basic economic infrastructure—such as feeder roads, railroads, telecommunication and ports—as well as the increased provision of basic social services, particularly in primary education and health. Such outlays are complementary to, rather than competitive with, private investment, thereby providing the needed support to private activity. A large part of the public investment program is financed by donor assistance. Under the program for 1990–92, the bulk of total planned investment resources (62 percent) continues to be allocated to the development of economic infrastructure, mainly in the energy, and roads and highways sectors. Some 22 percent of resources are devoted to directly productive sectors, comprising mostly resources for the development of agricultural infrastructure and the promotion of agricultural support services, as well as the improvement of key installations in the industrial and mining sectors. An increasing share of public investment (14 percent) is allocated to the support of the social and administrative sectors, mainly for the expanded and improved provision of health and education services. Nonetheless, notwithstanding the progress made in improving the economic infrastructure, much more remains to be done. In the area of the transportation network in particular, the World Bank staff estimates that it will take another 5 to 10 years of rehabilitation to restore Ghana's economic infrastructure to the level it was in the early 1970s.

The Government has been hampered in its ability to attain its expenditure goals completely by the fact that revenue, as a percentage of GDP, has fallen short of budgeted levels in each year since 1986; while revenue targets have been met in absolute terms, higher-than-expected inflation has led to higher nominal GDP and thus, lower revenue-to-GDP ratios. This suggests that Ghana's tax structure may not be very responsive to inflation. In 1990, for instance, a rapid increase in petroleum prices affected the general price level both directly as well as through its impact on transport costs (see Section VI). However, the price increases were not reflected in higher sales tax collections, as sales tax is collected at the wholesale level, thus excluding much of the transport costs. In addition, in periods of inflation, the real value of government revenue tends to be eroded by collection lags.[21] Choudhry (1991) esti-

mates that Ghana's real revenue has been reduced by approximately 5 percent a year owing to these lags.[22] Revenue shortfalls as a percentage of GDP have, in turn, required controls on both current and capital expenditure. While these controls have allowed the targets for the budget balance to be met, they might have led to inefficient spending patterns, with those categories of spending most easily controlled in the short run bearing the brunt of expenditure reductions.

With the recorded slowdown in recent years in government revenue, increased emphasis has been placed on enhancing the efficiency and effectiveness of the government expenditure programs. The long period of economic decline in the 1970s and early 1980s has led to a deterioration in the effectiveness of public expenditure management. In particular, expenditure control has become overly centralized, directed almost exclusively at financial control as opposed to monitoring and evaluating program effectiveness. Since 1986, progress has been made in rationalizing the budgetary procedures with technical assistance from the Fund and the World Bank; further improvements, particularly in the evaluation of the cost-effectiveness of specific programs, are currently being pursued.

Fiscal Balance and Government Savings

While both government revenue and expenditure have risen over the period 1983–90, implying that the role of the Government in the economy has expanded, an important measure of both the extent of adjustment and the impact of fiscal policy on the economy is the fiscal deficit. There are several measures of this deficit employed in Ghana; first, it is measured excluding capital expenditure financed by external project aid—the narrow deficit—or including this expenditure—the broad deficit. In addition, both the narrow and broad deficit are measured including and excluding grants as revenue (see Box 3 for a discussion of these various measures).[23]

In 1982, Ghana was running a narrow deficit equal to 6.3 percent of GDP. This was reduced sharply to 2.7 percent of GDP the following year, owing to the expenditure controls noted above.[24]

---

[21]See Tanzi (1977) for a general discussion of this issue.

[22]Choudhry (1991) has estimated the impact of collection lags on revenue for 18 developing countries during 1970–88. The estimated revenue erosion for Ghana was found to be greater than that of 14 of these countries.

[23]These measures of fiscal balance reflect the position of the Central Government only and exclude the net financial position of the Bank of Ghana and state-owned enterprises.

[24]As grants were trivial at this time, the fiscal deficit measured with or without grants as revenue was the same.

The narrow deficit (including grants) shifted into a surplus in 1986, which grew to 0.7 percent of GDP by 1989, before declining to an estimated 0.2 percent of GDP by 1990 (Table 10). Program grants, which were virtually nonexistent in 1983, have become an important source of revenue, reaching 1.5 percent of GDP by 1990, facilitating a higher level of domestic spending while enabling the achievement of the targets for the narrow balance. The broad deficit (including grants), on the other hand, remained fairly stable during 1983–90, fluctuating between 2.1 percent and 3.3 percent of GDP. The broad deficit reflects the heightened importance of capital expenditure financed by external project aid over this period. The broad deficit, excluding grants, has widened more or less steadily as a percentage of GDP over the period, rising to 5.5 percent in 1990, partly as a result of the declining share of grants in total project-related aid.

Reductions in the narrow fiscal deficit over time, as well as the availability of concessional foreign financing, have allowed the Government to reduce its recourse to net domestic borrowing and to make, since 1987, large net repayments to the banking system; these repayments amounted on average to the equivalent of 1.2 percent of GDP a year during 1987–90. The reduced demands by the Government on domestic financial resources have allowed, within a restrictive overall credit policy, a sizable expansion in real terms of credit to the private sector. In addition, the Government contributed 0.8 percent of GDP toward the cost of financial sector reform in 1990.

The fiscal deficits incurred by the Government of Ghana over the period 1983–90 were, in any case, quite small by comparison with other comparable countries. In 1990, countries in sub-Saharan Africa experienced on average a broad fiscal deficit, including grants, of nearly 8 percent of GDP, while the average deficit for all African countries exceeded 6 percent of GDP.

A major goal of economic policies since 1983 has been to raise national savings and investment, and achieving higher government savings has been an important component of this effort. The role of public savings is particularly important in such countries as Ghana, in which the real rate of return on private savings has generally been negative. Government savings,[25] which were negative at the beginning of the economic recovery program, rose as a ratio to GDP through the late 1980s, but have declined in the last several years. Savings, excluding grants, increased steadily, becoming positive

in 1985 and rising to nearly 3 percent of GDP by 1987 before falling to less than 2 percent of GDP by 1990. The overall growth in government savings over time has resulted from both the increase in tax revenue as a proportion of GDP, as well as the shift in the composition of expenditure from current to capital spending through 1988.

A broader view of government savings, consistent with national accounts estimates, would consider revenue from all sources, including external grants for investment projects. This broad measure of government savings also increased steadily through the period, reaching 5.6 percent of GDP in 1989, before declining to 4.9 percent in 1990. The 1991 budget provides for a sharp increase in broad-based government savings to 3.6 percent of GDP, excluding grants, and to 6.8 percent of GDP, including grants. This expansion is attributable primarily to an expected strong increase in Ghana's tax to GDP ratio, largely as a result of a marked expansion in petroleum tax revenue.

Trends in Revenue

Since 1983, tax revenue has risen as a proportion of GDP, reaching a peak of 12.7 percent in 1987, before declining to 11.6 percent in 1990 (Table 8). This increase reflected the combined effects of tax policy changes, improvements in tax administration and enforcement, and expansion of the tax base brought about by economic growth and changes in relative prices, particularly the exchange rate. Despite these gains, Ghana's revenue/GDP ratio is still low in comparison with that of other developing countries. Total government revenue amounted to 15.8 percent of GDP in 1990 including project grants, compared with nearly 24 percent for Africa as a whole, and 19 percent for sub-Saharan Africa.

The composition of tax revenue has changed significantly over the period of the economic recovery program; individual income taxation and export taxes now generate a significantly smaller share of revenue than in 1983, while corporate income tax and indirect taxes on imports and domestic goods account for a larger proportion of revenue.

Taxes on individual income fell from 8.6 percent of total revenue in 1983 to 6.5 percent in 1990, reflecting the sizable adjustments in the tax brackets and personal allowances made during 1987–89. As a result, the effective average tax rate declined for all income groups between 1986 and 1989. The relative importance of corporate income tax revenue, on the other hand, grew sharply in the mid-1980s before weakening in the

---

[25]Government savings are measured as total revenue less current expenditure and special efficiency spending.

Box 3. Measures of the Fiscal Deficit

The official budget of Ghana is constructed on a "narrow" basis, that is, excluding capital expenditure financed through external project aid, as well as the corresponding project grants and loans, but including foreign program grants. This has been done largely for reasons of administrative simplicity, but the calculation of the narrow budget can also be justified on the grounds that these capital outlays are financed by concessional foreign resources and have a large import content, and so have only a limited impact on aggregate domestic demand. Nonetheless, the narrow budget understates the impact of fiscal policy on economic activity, and the balance of payments. To compensate for these limitations, a "broad" deficit has also been calculated, including capital expenditure financed through external project aid. It is envisaged that following improvements in data collection and budgetary procedures, the Government will soon begin to formulate the budget on a broad basis.

The narrow and broad deficit measures can each be calculated either including or excluding foreign grants, that is, grants can be considered as either revenue or financing. In the case of the narrow deficit, external project grants are, by definition, always excluded; however, program grants may either be included or not. It can be argued that the deficit excluding grants reflects most accurately the extent of domestic fiscal adjustment; this view, however, would imply that grants mostly represent support for expenditure or programs that would have taken place whether or not the grants had been received. Another argument for excluding grants is that they may not be a stable or at least easily predictable source of revenue, and so they should not be treated in the same manner as government revenue more directly under the control of the Government, such as tax receipts.

---

last two years. The share of corporate tax revenue doubled, from just under 9 percent of total revenue in 1983 to 18 percent in 1988, owing in large part to a strengthening in company profitability and major improvements in tax administration. More recently, tax rate reductions and more important, a weakening in company profitability and sizable provisions for nonperforming assets made by banks, have led to a decline in the share of corporate tax receipts in total revenue, to 12.7 percent by 1990. In addition, the corporate tax continues to have a narrow base; only a few private and public enterprises incur any corporate tax liability.

Since the mid-1980s, declines in the share of excise taxes (other than petroleum excises) in total revenue have been offset by increases in the share of general sales tax receipts. As indicated above, the coverage of excise taxes has become more narrow over time and, in addition, the domestic production of those goods still subject to excise tax—tobacco and alcoholic beverages—has stagnated in the last several years. Thus, the taxation of goods and services has shifted from taxes on specific goods to a wide variety of domestically produced goods.[26] At the same time, receipts from excise taxes on petroleum products, introduced in 1985, increased dramatically, from only 1.5 percent of total revenue in 1985 to 9.5 percent in 1990.

---

[26]Exemptions from the general sales tax include food (raw and prepared), educational materials, machinery and equipment used in agriculture, manufacturing and mining, petroleum products, and exported goods. It should be noted that the sales tax is applied at the wholesale level.

A major shift also took place during 1983–90 in the structure and importance of taxes on international trade. The overall share in total revenue of taxes on international trade has declined, reflecting main reductions in the share of cocoa export tax receipts, which fell from 35.3 percent of total revenue in 1983 to 10.2 percent by 1990. The share of import duties, on the other hand, has risen over the same period.

Finally, with the increasing confidence by donors in Ghana's economic policies, foreign grants have grown as a proportion of total government revenue, rising from less than 1 percent in 1983 to more than 10 percent in 1990.

Trends in Expenditure

Total government expenditure and net lending (narrow coverage) rose steadily from 8.2 percent of GDP in 1983 to 14.4 percent in 1989, before declining to 14.0 percent of GDP in 1990 (Table 9). The general increase in spending over time has reflected the increased emphasis attached to developing and rehabilitating the economic and social infrastructure and, more recently, to ensuring that the benefits of adjustment are broadly shared. Partly as a result of spending for Ghana's participation in a peace-keeping force in Liberia and for a conference of the Non-Aligned Movement planned for September 1991, the budget for 1991 provides for a resumption of growth in government expenditure in relation to GDP, with total spending expected to reach 14.5 percent of GDP.

There was a significant shift in the composition of expenditure over this period. The share of current expenditure in total spending declined, as the share of both interest payments and subsidies and transfers fell. Interest payments declined between 1986 and 1988, from 15.5 to 8.0 percent of total spending, reflecting the shift of the narrow budget balance into surplus.[27] In 1990, however, spending on interest increased, owing in part to the assumption of responsibility by the Government for foreign interest payments due from certain state-owned enterprises experiencing financial difficulties, and the replacement of the Bank of Ghana's revaluation losses outstanding at the end of 1989 with government bonds.

Subsidies and transfers, which comprised 27 percent of expenditure in 1983, now account for just 10 percent. Direct subsidies to state-owned enterprises have been virtually eliminated, as part of a general push by the Government to enhance the efficiency and performance of the state enterprise sector. However, while data are sketchy, it nevertheless appears that the Central Government still provides significant indirect support to state enterprises through concessional interest rates on loans on-lent to enterprises, government guarantees on foreign loans to state enterprises, and arrears on taxes and charges for government services.

The state enterprise sector in Ghana comprises some 200 enterprises, which account for a large part of the activity in the mining, manufacturing, utility, transportation, and services sectors and employ a sizable segment of the labor force. While a few of these enterprises are profitable, most are characterized by major financial and structural weaknesses, including overstaffing. An improvement in the efficiency and profitability of the state enterprise sector and a reduction of its demand for financial and managerial resources from the Government have been the basic objectives of the state enterprise reform program pursued, with assistance from the World Bank, since 1987. For a number of reasons, progress in implementing this reform program was initially slow, but has gained momentum since 1990. By early 1991, some 40 state enterprises have been divested, while for several major enterprises that are slated to remain in the Government's portfolio a number of steps have been taken to strengthen their financial position and monitor their performance, including the preparation of rolling three-

year corporate plans and the signing of annual performance agreements with the Government. In addition, efforts are under way to liberalize the administrative and institutional environment within which state enterprises operate so as to improve their autonomy and accountability, as well as prepare financial accounts for as many enterprises as possible. Notwithstanding these efforts, much more remains to be done, particularly in divesting some profitable state enterprises.

Outlays on wages and salaries increased dramatically, from 19.2 percent to 35.7 percent of total spending during 1984–86, but their share declined through 1989. A one-time rise in wage and transportation allowances granted for the last two months of 1990, equivalent to 45 percent of basic pay a month, led to a slight increase in the share of wages and salaries for the year. Spending under the special efficiency program, introduced in 1987, has accounted for between 2.0 percent and 4.7 percent of total expenditure over the past four years. In each year since its inception, however, there has been a lower-than-budgeted level of special efficiency expenditure, reflecting both problems in implementation, as well as the fact that the special efficiency budget has been controlled in response to revenue shortfalls.[28]

Capital spending in the narrow budget accounted for less than 8 percent of total expenditure in 1983; this share increased to nearly 20 percent in 1988, before falling slightly in the past two years. As a percentage of GDP, capital expenditure rose from 0.6 percent to 2.5 percent over this period; including externally financed projects, the increase was even more dramatic, from 0.6 percent to 5.0 percent of GDP.

From the point of view of the functional classification of government expenditure, there has been a considerable shift in the activities supported by government expenditure since 1983. In particular, there has been a decline in the share of total expenditure accounted for by general public services, economic services, and defense.[29] The importance of expenditure on economic services to agriculture, mining, and manufacturing declined through 1988, but agriculture's share rose in 1989. The share of expenditure on roads dropped dramatically in 1986 and 1987, but has since expanded

---

[27]For liquidity management purposes, the net repayments by the Government to the banking system were only in part reflected in the outstanding stock of domestic government debt.

[28]Special efficiency expenditure represents essentially current rather than capital spending; thus presenting it as a separate spending category tends to overstate the extent to which the share of current expenditure in total spending has declined, although the general trend is downward whether it is included as current spending or not.

[29]Data for 1990 and budget data for 1991 are not yet available on a functional basis.

substantially. It is likely that this recent increase in spending on roads largely benefits agriculture as it reflects a greater emphasis on the construction of feeder roads in rural areas, which reduce transport costs for farmers, enhance efficiency, and support rural incomes. Spending on education, health, and social security and welfare has, over the same period, expanded steadily, with important implications for the well-being of the poor (see below).

According to official statistics, defense expenditure, after rising from 4.6 percent of total spending in 1983 to 7.5 percent in 1985, fell steadily thereafter to 3.1 percent of total spending by 1989. In relation to GDP, defense expenditure fell from 1.0 percent in 1985 to 0.4 percent in 1989. By either measure, Ghana's military spending is low by international standards; for all developing countries, in 1988 such spending amounted on average to 13.1 percent of total government expenditure and to 2.7 percent of GDP.

Fiscal Policy and Social Welfare

One important aspect of fiscal policy is the extent to which it has aided the poorest members of the society and promoted a broader distribution of the benefits from adjustment. Poverty in Ghana is largely a rural phenomenon, with nearly 80 percent of poor households[30] living in the rural areas, and with the poorest of the poor concentrated in rural areas as well. Thus, public expenditure policy can improve the well-being of the poor either by providing services consumed in large part by the poor, or by channeling goods and services to rural areas. In addition, tax policy influences the distribution of income both directly by changing relative tax burdens and indirectly via the impact on incentives to work, save, and invest.

Government Expenditure and Social Welfare Policy

Data limitations make it difficult to measure precisely the impact of fiscal policy on income distribution and the well-being of the poor.[31] It is clear, however, that the Government has intensified its efforts to aid the poorest groups in Ghana, as well as those most adversely affected by structural adjustment. These two groups are not identical and may, in fact, be quite different; for

instance, among those made worse off over the past seven years are laid-off public sector employees, who are not particularly poor relative to the general population, while many relatively poor small farmers producing tradable goods have been made significantly better off by the increases in real producer prices.

The extent to which government expenditure policy has addressed the social needs of the society can be gauged by examining the level of resources directed toward education, health, and social security and welfare. As indicated below, health and education services are not currently consumed disproportionately by the poor; however, such consumption may be determined primarily by access. In any case, provision of such services represents a means for many households to escape poverty. Government spending on these three categories increased from 2.3 percent of GDP in 1983 to 5.8 percent of GDP in 1989, and from 29.1 percent of total government expenditure in 1983 to 41.7 percent in 1989 (Table 11). In effect, increased social welfare spending has been made possible by a combination of enhanced revenue mobilization and declines in interest payments and subsidies, primarily to state enterprises.

Measuring the social welfare element of fiscal policy in this simple way is, however, problematic. First, much spending on education, health, and social security and welfare does not benefit the needy. For instance, spending on higher education typically benefits the relatively wealthy, as does some health expenditure on categories other than basic care. It would be preferable to consider only the outlays for primary education and basic health care, both in aggregate and by geographic region, but such data are not available.

Although the figures cited above tend to overstate the extent to which government expenditure aids the poor, they still provide evidence of an increase in such aid over time, assuming that the share of such spending benefiting the poor has not declined significantly during the period. In fact, the Government has been focusing on increasing the provision of primary education and basic health care services. For instance, since 1987 the share of primary education in the recurrent budget of the Ministry of Education has increased from 40 percent to 43 percent, and primary school enrollment is estimated to have risen from 65 percent to 72 percent. The Government is in the process of instituting a number of improvements in the procedures for budget planning and monitoring, in part to allow the collection of more detailed information on the composition of spending, and thus facilitate a strengthening of the poverty focus of government expenditure.

---

[30]A household is defined here as poor if its income is less than two thirds of the national average. See Boateng and others (1990) for a detailed discussion.

[31]For earlier study of the impact of adjustment on poverty, see Heller and others (1988).

Table 11. Central Government Social Welfare Expenditure, 1975–89

	1975	1980	1983	1984	1985	1986	1987	1988	1989
					(In percent of GDP)				
Narrow measure[1]	8.7	5.9	2.3	3.3	4.4	5.2	5.3	5.7	5.8
Broad measure[2]	9.5	6.5	2.6	3.7	4.8	5.7	6.2	6.7	7.1
					(In percent of total central government expenditure)				
Narrow measure[1]	39.9	30.6	29.1	33.0	32.8	37.6	38.6	41.5	41.7
Broad measure[2]	43.8	33.7	32.5	37.4	36.3	41.2	45.2	48.6	51.2

Source: Data provided by the Ghanaian authorities.
[1] Includes expenditure on education, health, and social security and welfare.
[2] Includes narrow measure plus spending on housing and community amenities, other community and social services, and special efficiency.

There is an additional element involved in estimating the social impact of government spending from the data presented above, namely, that some spending that benefits the poor or those adversely affected by adjustment is excluded from the categories of education, health, and social security and welfare. For instance, the special efficiency budget for retraining and supporting redeployed public sector employees can be seen as part of a general effort to provide a safety net and to spread more broadly the benefits of adjustment. In addition, expenditure on housing and community amenities, as well as other community and social services, provides substantial benefits to the poor and disadvantaged. Including these categories provides a broader measure of social welfare spending; such spending was raised from 2.6 percent of GDP in 1983 to 7.1 percent in 1989; as a percentage of total government expenditure, the increase was equally dramatic: from 32.5 percent to 51.2 percent.

Finally, the Government has also put into place, beginning in early 1988, the largely donor-financed Program of Actions to Mitigate the Social Costs of Adjustment, or PAMSCAD. At its inception, PAMSCAD was projected to cost some US$85 million. Through the end of 1990, however, actual disbursements have been just 4.6 billion cedis, significantly less than the 9.1 billion cedis allocated in the public investment program. The complexity of the program, which includes a large number of projects across various sectors of the economy, and many with multiple donors, appears to have slowed the pace of implementation. As a result, the Government plans to focus on a small number of priority areas, including community initiative projects, hand-dug wells and low-cost sanitation, agricultural credit, supplementary feeding for malnourished children, and nonformal education.

Taxation and Income Distribution

The incidence, or burden, of the change in the tax structure during the 1983–90 period is difficult to measure. To begin with, there is the conceptual difficulty of the baseline, or counterfactual, against which the changes are to be measured. Since both the level and distribution of taxation have changed, it is not appropriate to simply compare tax payments by particular groups over time. More relevant is the question of how is the current distribution of the tax burden different from the one that would have resulted from an equally large expansion of tax revenues that maintained the original 1983 distribution of revenues by type of tax. An analysis of changes in the share of total revenue raised by different taxes would allow a rough approximation of changes in the distribution of income owing to tax changes. However, revenue raised from some sources, such as corporate income, may increase despite reductions in effective tax rates, if economic growth or changes in relative prices lead to an expansion in the tax base. Increased tax payments generated by such base expansion have different distributional implications than, for example, increased rates levied on a fixed base.

Despite these complications, it is possible to describe several broad changes during the period under consideration. First, as noted, personal income taxation has fallen as a proportion of total revenue, particularly since 1986, largely as a result of upward adjustments to income tax brackets and personal allowances. Effective tax rates have declined for all income groups; in addition, it appears that the overall effect of this tax change has been mildly progressive. Between 1986 and the 1991 budget, those with real taxable income of between 10,000–20,000 cedis were removed from income tax rolls completely, while those with in-

Table 12. Expenditure Patterns by Poverty Group[1]
(In percent of total expenditure)

	Non-poor	Poor
Expenditure on food	43.9	36.1
Consumption of home-produced food	22.2	33.0
Consumption of home-produced nonfood	1.9	1.7
Other consumer expenditure of which:	28.1	27.0
Gasoline	0.4	0.0
Other fuel	1.2	2.0
Public transportation	1.7	1.3
Cigarettes, tobacco	1.0	1.9
Housing	1.2	1.5
Medical services	1.5	1.7
Education	2.4	2.3
Other expenditures[2]	3.9	2.2

Source: Boateng and others (1990).
[1]Based on a 1988 survey.
[2]Includes remittances paid out and expenditure corresponding to in-kind employment income.

come of 30,000 cedis have seen a decline of over 60 percent in their average effective rate.[32] However, it is unclear how many taxpayers have been affected by these changes; many of the poorest members of society do not pay income taxes, as they engage in subsistence farming or in activities in the informal sector. These individuals have been untouched by income tax policy changes. The average tax rate for the highest-income taxpayers changed relatively little over the period; for those earning over 5 million cedis, for instance, the average tax rate declined by only 6 percent, as most of their taxable income remains at the highest marginal tax rate.

Since the 1991 budget was announced, new changes in the personal income tax have taken place; allowances paid to public and private sector employees are, as of July 1991, included in the income tax base, while marginal rates have been lowered considerably, to between 5 and 25 percent. This change has been designed to be revenue neutral and, by lowering effective marginal rates, may increase incentives to work and save. However, it may have a somewhat regressive impact on the income tax structure; as some allowances are paid as a flat amount, they comprise a larger share of the total earnings of lower-income employees than of those at the top end of the pay scale.[33] On

the other hand, increases in personal allowances should in part offset this adverse effect.

Second, petroleum taxes have increased dramatically over the past several years. This trend places a larger tax burden on those consumers who buy a proportionately large quantity of petroleum products, either directly or indirectly (e.g., through transportation costs), as well as those with either capital or labor employed in the production of goods that use a great deal of petroleum. It is difficult to determine precisely who bears the burden of the petroleum tax, although there is no evidence that the poor are particularly large consumers of petroleum products. The poor purchase almost no gasoline and actually spend a smaller proportion of their income on public transportation than do the non-poor (Table 12). They do, however, spend a greater share of their income on other fuels, such as kerosene, the tax on which has also been raised. Food prices are also affected by the higher transportation costs. The poor actually spend a smaller share of their income on food, consuming a greater proportion of home-produced food. Thus, higher food prices need not primarily affect the poor as a group, although the urban poor, who are likely to spend a large proportion of their income on food, would probably be hard hit. In addition, many of the poor are farmers, whose costs increase with higher petroleum prices.

Third, excise taxes have become less important, while the role of general sales tax has increased. This shift tends to favor those who consume more of the excisable items, namely cigarettes and beer, most likely the poor. However, this change has come about largely as a result of decreased

[32]Figures for 1991 are based on projected changes in the consumer price index.

[33]Note that there is an inherent trade-off between attempts to increase after-tax wage relativities in the public sector and increasing the progressivity of the personal income tax system.

production in the affected industries, rather than via rate reductions. The reduction in the sales tax rate in the 1991 budget is likely to have a progressive impact on the overall tax structure. Although the tax is imposed at the wholesale level, it is likely that final consumers bear much of the actual tax burden. Since the proportion of income consumed by households typically declines with income, the poor would tend to benefit the most from reductions in consumption taxes. It may be argued that this tendency would be offset somewhat by the fact that food is exempt from the general sales tax; however, as noted, the poor actually spend a significantly smaller portion of their income on food than do the non-poor.

Fourth, the share of corporate income taxation in total revenue rose through 1988, but has fallen since then. Recent reductions in corporate tax rates may have a regressive impact on the tax system, although if they are successful in generating additional private investment, real wages could eventually rise, with further positive distributional implications. Again, to the extent that changes are driven by exogenous expansion or contraction of the tax base, they are not, in and of themselves, evidence of changes in tax burden, as measured by changes in effective tax rates.

Fifth, the decline in cocoa taxes reflects mainly a decision by the Government to increase producer prices paid to cocoa farmers. Thus, it is clear that these farmers have been made better off by the change in tax structure. What is less clear, however, is the relative position in the income distribution held by cocoa producers.

Conclusions

This section has examined fiscal adjustment in Ghana since 1983, which aimed at correcting fiscal imbalances, improving the economic infrastructure, and ensuring that the benefits of adjustment have been broadly shared. The process has been largely a success, although difficulties remain. The fiscal deficit, including foreign grants, generally declined over 1983–90; in recent years, this decline, along with the availability of substantial concessional foreign financing, has allowed significant net repayments by the Government to the domestic banking system. Government savings (including grants) rose between 1983 and 1989, before declining somewhat in 1990. Recently, tax policy has been aimed at enhancing the incentives for investment and savings by the private sector.

The tax-to-GDP ratio rose up to 1987, although this trend was partly reversed in 1988–90. Ghana's revenue-to-GDP ratio remains low compared with that in other African countries and with developing countries elsewhere. A major change in the tax structure has taken place as well. The tax system has shifted from a heavy reliance on taxes on international trade to greater use of taxes on domestic goods and services; in particular, the share of cocoa export taxes has declined over time, while the general sales tax and petroleum taxes have come to play an important role. Taxes on corporate income have grown as a share of total revenue since 1983, while the share of personal income tax revenue has declined.

Capital expenditure rose as a share of total government spending over the period, reflecting the goal of rehabilitating the economic infrastructure, although this share has declined slightly during the last two years. The Government has made an effort to spread more broadly the benefits of adjustment; spending on social welfare has expanded during the period, both as a share of GDP and as a share of total expenditure. In addition, a number of the changes in the tax structure since 1983 have had positive implications for low-income households.

While some aspects of the improvement in the fiscal position appear to have slowed in the past two or three years, the 1991 budget is designed to regain the momentum. In particular, the fiscal balance is projected to improve in 1991, allowing greater government savings and further net repayments to the banking system. The 1991 budget provides for a large increase in the tax-to-GDP ratio, reflecting sharp hikes in petroleum tax rates during 1990. In addition, reforms in the taxation of capital income, announced in the 1991 budget, have been designed to improve the incentives to save and invest.

VI Monetary Policy and Inflation

Financial discipline in Ghana in the years prior to 1983 was weak. Large fiscal deficits had resulted in high rates of growth of domestic credit and broad money, fueling inflation, widening the spread between the official and parallel market exchange rates, and exacerbating the external imbalances. Furthermore, some measures taken in the early 1980s to eliminate fraud (including the freezing of certain bank deposits pending investigation for tax liability) had weakened public confidence in the banking system and resulted in a large switch of bank deposits into currency outside banks; by the end of 1983, the share of currency outside banks in total broad money had risen to 47 percent. In this context, the rate of inflation had accelerated by the early 1980s; averaging more than 70 percent during 1980–83, and interest rates had become substantially negative in real terms, while the financial health of the banking system had been severely weakened by the prolonged period of economic decline.

Monetary policies since 1983 have initially focused on quantitative credit controls, with only modest efforts to liberalize the policy environment and strengthen the regulatory and institutional framework. Since late 1989, however, a major impetus was given to shifting to a market-oriented system of monetary control, as well as the restructuring of the banking system. In the event, credit policy has been broadly restrictive, supporting the liberalization of the exchange and trade system. However, for most of the period since 1983 the growth in broad money remained high and the progress in absorbing the excess liquidity from the economy was slow, owing in large part to a number of rigidities in the banking system. Inflation, although it has declined sharply, remained at unacceptably high levels. In response, monetary policies since late 1989 have focused primarily on bringing inflation under control through an enhancement of the effectiveness of liquidity management and the monetary transmission mechanisms. As a result of these efforts, nominal interest rates rose in late 1990 and the first half of 1991 to levels that are for the most part significantly positive in real terms, while inflation fell to less than 20 percent in the year to May 1991.

Although monetary developments are an important determinant of price movements, other factors have also exerted a strong influence on changes in the general price level. In the context of the Ghanaian economy, developments in consumer prices appear to be influenced by three kinds of factors: first, exogenous shocks in the domestic food supply; second, domestic and external cost-push factors, including changes in the exchange rate, import prices, wages, and administered prices; and third, demand-pull factors arising from developments in domestic demand and the stance of macroeconomic policies. This chapter reviews monetary policies and developments in Ghana since 1983 and focuses on an analysis of the main determinants of inflation, with particular emphasis on the contribution of supply and cost-push factors.

Monetary Developments and Policies

Monetary policies under Ghana's economic recovery program have been primarily directed at regaining control of credit expansion by the banking system, particularly to the Government, while at the same time supporting the exchange rate policy and achieving the targets for real output growth, inflation, and the overall balance of payments position. Over time, as the immediate adjustment needs of the economy were addressed, the focus of monetary policies was broadened to encompass greater emphasis on the liberalization of controls on interest rates and bank credit and a gradual shift to an indirect system of monetary control. These policies were complemented by a major program of financial sector reform, supported by the World Bank, aimed at enhancing the soundness of the banking system by improving the regulatory framework and strengthening bank supervision, and at improving the efficiency and profitability of banks, including replacing of their nonperforming assets. Appendix I describes the financial system in Ghana and reviews the main aspects of the program of financial sector reform. To accelerate the process of financial deepening and the mobilization of financial savings, policies have also focused on restoring positive real interest rates and increasing the access, and availability, of a broad range of financial instruments to individual investors.

During 1983–86, monetary policies were directed at lowering the Government's net recourse to financing from the domestic banking system, contributing to an overall slowdown in credit and monetary expansion. To this end, the Bank of Ghana has relied on quantitative controls in the form of ceilings on the net domestic assets of the banking system and net bank credit to the Government and the Cocoa Board, so as to avoid crowding out the financing needs of the private sector. At the operational level, these aggregate ceilings were enforced through quarterly credit ceilings for individual banks. Given the state of Ghana's financial system at the time and the limited availability of monetary instruments, the reliance on quantitative credit controls, despite their well-recognized limitations for the efficiency of financial intermediation, was largely unavoidable. With the marked improvement in government finances, this policy was generally successful.[34] The administrative controls on bank interest rates were maintained, but the level of interest rates was raised somewhat in discrete steps while inflation was coming down.

From late 1987 to mid-1989, the focus of monetary policies was broadened to include, besides the observance of credit ceilings, the gradual dismantling of administrative interest rate and credit controls. To this end, the limits on the maximum bank lending rates and the minimum bank term deposit rates were lifted in September 1987, while the controls on the minimum bank savings deposit rate were liberalized in February 1988. Similarly, the controls on the sectoral allocation of bank credit were abolished in February 1988, except for a minimum requirement for loans to the agricultural sector which was finally lifted in November 1990. The rate of growth in net domestic credit decelerated from 61 percent in 1985 to 13 percent in

1988, reflecting largely the continued improvement in government finances and, in particular, the switch to sizable net repayments by the Government to the banking system from 1987 onward (Chart 7 and Table 13). These repayments facilitated a more moderate slowdown in private sector credit within a restrictive overall credit policy. Nonetheless, larger-than-expected inflows of external concessional assistance and the associated stronger-than-expected improvement in the balance of payments contributed to a rapid expansion in broad money until 1988. Although the growth in money supply decelerated from a peak of 72 percent in 1984 to 43 percent by the end of 1988, it exceeded the targets in the Government's monetary program and the growth in nominal GDP.

Efforts to sterilize the monetary impact of the strong improvement in the net foreign assets position of the Bank of Ghana were only partially successful, given the rudimentary development of the money market in Ghana at the time and the lack of appropriate financial instruments, thus augmenting the existing excess liquidity in the economy. In the face of increasing excess bank cash reserves and the limited incentives to mobilize new deposits, given the binding credit ceilings, the banks responded to the lifting of controls on interest rates by lowering their deposit rates, thus raising further their already large interest rate margins. The credit ceilings, together with the accumulation of a large stock of nonperforming assets, had aggravated the rigidities in the banking system, by reducing the flexibility to provide bank credit to new and potentially more dynamic customers, notwithstanding the ongoing changes in the sectoral composition of real output. The financial sector reform program, introduced in early 1988, began to alleviate these constraints essentially from 1990 onward, given the time needed to complete the necessary preparatory work.

The increasing monetization of the economy and the gradually improving confidence in the banking system are estimated to have contributed to an increase in the demand for money at a rate higher than the growth in nominal GDP during the period 1983–88, consistent with a declining velocity of circulation. However, the expansion in money supply during this period exceeded the estimated increase in the demand for money. Nonetheless, the weak development of financial markets in Ghana and the associated high transaction costs seem to have limited the ability of economic agents to quickly dispose of any "undesired" build-up of money balances, thus contributing to the emergence of excess liquidity in the economy,

---

[34]Nevertheless, owing to a major broadening of the coverage of the monetary accounts to include, in addition to the three primary commercial banks, the operations of seven secondary banks, the recorded credit and monetary expansion during 1984–85 accelerated significantly, largely as a result of the inclusion of transactions previously excluded from monetary statistics; for example the growth of broad money increased from 38 percent in 1983 to 60 percent in 1985.

Chart 7. Monetary Developments

Sources: Data provided by the Ghanaian authorities.
[1]Owing to a major broadening of the coverage of the monetary accounts in 1984, comparable data are not available for earlier years.
[2]Excluding the takeover by the Government in 1990 of the revaluation losses of the Bank of Ghana.
[3]Including the revaluation account.

Table 13. Monetary Developments and Inflation, 1983–91
(Annual percentage changes)

	Broad Money[1]	Currency Outside Banks	Net Domestic Assets Banking System[2,3]	Net Domestic Credit[3]	Credit to the Non-Government Sector	Nominal GDP	Velocity of Circulation[4]	Consumer Prices (Average data)
1983	38.1	49.3	41.2	35.0	−43.7	112.9	9.0	122.8
1984	72.1	69.7	76.5	63.1	295.8	47.0	7.7	39.6
1985	59.5	27.9	68.2	60.8	128.3	26.8	6.1	10.4
1986	53.7	43.4	41.8	33.8	50.8	49.1	5.9	24.6
1987	53.0	51.4	10.8	5.6	20.8	45.9	5.6	39.8
1988	43.0	38.6	10.7	12.7	30.3	40.9	5.6	31.4
1989	26.9	27.5	−17.4	−3.0	12.0	34.8	5.9	25.2
1990	18.0	−3.5	−48.9	8.9	28.7	33.5	6.7	37.2
1991[5]	19.1	−2.2	−1.7	10.3	34.9	...	...	24.6

Sources: Data provided by the Ghanaian authorities; and IMF staff estimates.

[1] The coverage of the monetary survey was broadened to include, in addition to the three commercial banks, the seven secondary banks since 1984 and the Consolidated Discount House since 1988; monetary and credit data are on an end-period basis.

[2] The large declines in 1989 and 1990 reflect a reclassification of the net foreign assets of the Bank of Ghana and of a major commercial bank.

[3] Excluding the takeover by the Government of the revaluation losses of the Bank of Ghana in 1990.

[4] Ratio of nominal GDP to end-period broad money.

[5] Latest available figures; the monetary data refer to April 1991, and consumer prices refer to the period up to May 1991.

mainly in the form of currency outside banks.[35] Surprisingly, no significant spillover of the excess money holdings into imports financed though the official banking system has been noted, although it is possible that the liquidity holdings boosted the demand for foreign exchange in the parallel foreign exchange market. The bloated holdings of broad money by the public have tended to accommodate the price effects of any unanticipated shocks (such as disturbances in domestic food supply) through changes in the velocity of circulation.

Building on the lessons from this experience, and prompted in part by the reemergence of inflationary pressures in mid-1989 and the rigidity of bank interest rates at levels that continued to be significantly negative in real terms, Ghana's monetary policies entered a new, more dynamic phase in late 1989, characterized by major policy and institutional reforms. The stance of monetary policy has since been tightened markedly, accompanied by the stepped-up implementation of the financial sector reform program and the introduction of a program of monetary policy reform. The latter reform involved the gradual phasing in of an indirect system of monetary control, entailing a shift away from direct controls toward increased reliance on market-based instruments of policy, thus allowing in due course the removal of credit ceilings. As part of this process, the Bank of Ghana rationalized the minimum cash and liquid reserve requirements for banks; introduced new financial instruments; intensified the absorption of excess liquidity from the economy through open market operations at market determined yields; and strengthened its monetary management capacity. In addition, the financial position of the Bank of Ghana was strengthened through the conversion of the revaluation losses accumulated by the end of September 1990 into long-term government bonds offering a yield sufficient to allow the Bank of Ghana to conduct its monetary policies without being impeded by considerations about its own profitability.[36]

As a result of these efforts, a large volume of excess liquidity was sterilized though the sale of non-rediscountable Bank of Ghana instruments and large net repayments by the Government to the Bank of Ghana; indicative of the scale of liquidity management operations is the fact that during the ten-month period to September 1990, the equivalent of about 12.5 percent of broad money was

---

[35] This development is characteristic of many developing countries, where in the absence of well established financial markets, adjustment to unexpected changes in the money supply primarily has to take place through the goods markets, which, however, takes time and may result in temporary excess cash balances (Khan (1980)).

[36] The reforms in Ghana's financial system since 1986 are summarized in Box 4. For the sequencing of financial liberalization in general, and the role of interest rate liberalization within such a process, see Villanueva and Mirakhor (1990) and Leite and Sundararajan (1990).

sterilized, contributing to a reduction in excess bank cash reserves to modest levels in relation to total bank deposits. In addition, the expansion in net domestic credit moderated further to 10 percent by early 1991, while the growth in broad money declined to 27 percent by the end of 1989 and 19 percent by April 1991. In annual average terms, the growth in broad money decelerated from 45 percent in 1988 to 34 percent in 1989 and 23 percent in 1990. In the latter year, monetary expansion was substantially lower than inflation and the growth in nominal GDP, implying a sharp decline in real terms as well as a marked increase in the average velocity of circulation. The growth in currency outside banks also slowed, indicative of the positive impact of liquidity management on financial intermediation, falling from 39 percent in 1988 to 28 percent in 1989, before actually turning negative in 1990 (3.5 percent); associated with this was an increasing share of demand deposits in money supply.[37]

Despite the large volume of open market operations and the slowdown in monetary expansion, money market interest rates rose only modestly until September 1990, while bank deposit and lending rates remained virtually unchanged at levels substantially negative in real terms; in contrast, the interest rates in the informal money market remained at rates in excess of 10 percent a month. At the same time, the inflation rate continued to increase. The limited responsiveness of interest rates to the tightening in domestic liquidity conditions reflected largely the existing rigidities in the banking system, as well as concerns by the Bank of Ghana about the impact of higher interest rates on its profitability and the balance sheet position of banks at a time when they were in the process of replacing their nonperforming assets. The banking system in Ghana was still characterized by limited competitiveness, a large degree of direct or indirect government control (the Government owns or controls 8 out of the 13 banks in the banking system), and a slow response as of then to the changing policy and institutional environment, reflecting perhaps the residual impact from the prolonged exposure to direct administrative controls.

The behavior of interest rates, together with the usual lags in the monetary transmission mecha-

nisms, the outstanding excess liquidity in the economy, and the increase in the velocity of circulation, weakened the impact of the deceleration in monetary aggregates on price developments until late 1990. In response to this limited effectiveness of monetary policies, a broad range of measures was introduced in late 1990 and early 1991, designed to strengthen the responsiveness of interest rates to changes in liquidity conditions. These measures included a phased increase in the Bank of Ghana's rediscount rate from 26 percent to 35 percent by early January 1991, a widening of the access to purchases of Bank of Ghana financial instruments to the nonbank sector, and several other measures to enhance the transparency and efficiency of open market operations. As a result of these policy changes, the annualized yields on money market instruments rose markedly from a range of 23–29 percent in September 1990 to 31–38 percent by mid-1991, inducing an upward adjustment in the structure of bank deposit and lending rates. In the face of increasing competition for deposits, given the very attractive returns of government and Bank of Ghana financial instruments, average bank deposit rates were raised from 15–20 percent in September 1990 to 18–23 percent by June 1991, while average bank lending rates were raised from 24–28 percent to 28–31 percent, respectively. With the marked reduction in the year-on-year inflation rate to less than 20 percent by May 1991, money market rates as well as bank lending rates and the bulk of bank deposit rates became significantly positive in real terms.

The banks have responded well to the increase in money market interest rates, by raising the attractiveness of their deposits (including special rates for individual big customers), improving the quality of their services, lowering somewhat their interest rate margins,[38] and intensifying their efforts to reduce their operating costs. Individual investors also responded well to the new investment opportunities opened to them, by converting some of their holdings of cash into bank deposits or money market placements, shifting in part away from activities in the informal money market. At the same time, the higher level of interest rates is reported to be having an increasing impact in the credit demand decisions by the private sector and the credit allocation decisions by banks, even though access to credit is still the principal factor underlying the expansion of credit to the private sector.

---

[37]By April 1991, the share of currency outside banks in total broad money, which can be considered as an (inverse) indicator for the degree of financial innovation (Arrau and others (1991)), had fallen to 28 percent. Nevertheless, this level is still high in comparison with other African countries; for example, in mid-1990 the share of currency outside banks amounted to 24 percent in Nigeria, 19 percent in Kenya, and 17 percent in Togo.

---

[38]These margins fell to about 9 percentage points, a level still high in comparison with neighboring countries; in Côte d'Ivoire they amount to some 7 percentage points and in Nigeria to 6 percentage points.

Box 4. Reforms in the Financial System, 1986–91

1986
September   Introduction of a weekly foreign exchange auction.

1987
September   Decontrol of maximum bank lending rates and minimum term deposit rates.
October   Introduction of a weekly auction for the sale of treasury bills.
November   Establishment of the Consolidated Discount House.

1988
February   Decontrol of minimum bank savings rate.
    Removal of sectoral credit controls, except for a minimum requirement for credit to the agricultural sector.
April   Establishment of foreign exchange bureaus.
September   Introduction of 90-day Bank of Ghana bills, available to banks.

1989
July   Adoption by the Government of a comprehensive restructuring plan for the banking sector.
August   Adoption of a revised banking law, strengthening the regulatory environment and bank supervision by the Bank of Ghana.
December   Introduction of nonrediscountable medium-term Bank of Ghana instruments with maturities of 180 days, 1 year, and 2 years, available to banks.

1990
January   Appointment of new management and boards of directors of financially distressed banks.
March   Unification of bank cash reserve requirements on demand and time and savings deposits.
April   Unification of the exchange markets (auction and bureau market).
    Commencement of implementation of restructuring plans for three financially distressed banks.
May   Replacement of nonperforming bank claims on state-owned enterprises, primarily with Bank of Ghana bonds.
November   Opening of a stock exchange.
    Introduction of 30-day Bank of Ghana bills and 180-day, 1-year and 2-year treasury bills, as well as new 5-year government stock.
    Widening of access to Bank of Ghana medium-term instruments to the nonbank sector.
    Abolition of the requirement for bank lending to the agricultural sector.
    Decontrol of all bank charges and fees.
    Reduction in the required bank cash reserves and increase in the required secondary reserves.
    Commencement of implementation of restructuring plans for three additional financially distressed banks.
December   Introduction of a 3 percent remuneration on bank cash deposits with the Bank of Ghana.
    Replacement of revaluation losses of the Bank of Ghana accumulated by end-September 1990 by long-term government bonds.
    Replacement of nonperforming claims on the private sector by the financially distressed banks, primarily with Bank of Ghana bonds.
    First compliance test based on new capital adequacy requirements.

1991
March   Finalization of the restructuring plan for the seventh distressed bank.
    Replacement of the nonperforming claims on the private sector by the four sound banks, primarily with Bank of Ghana bonds.
June   Opening of a second discount house (Securities Discount House).
July   Further reduction in the bank cash reserve requirement and increase in the secondary reserve requirement, together with a modification of the eligible reserve assets.
    Increase in the rate of remuneration on bank cash deposits with the Bank of Ghana to 5 percent.

Developments in Prices

An overview of Ghana's inflation performance during the 1980s leads to two main observations. First, the inflation rate has declined significantly, from an average annual rate of 73 percent in the early 1980s to about 25 percent in the first five months of 1991. In fact, the percentage increase in the consumer price index between December 1990 and May 1991 was lower than in all preceding years since the introduction of the economic recovery program. Second, annual average inflation rates exhibited sizable swings: after a drop to 10 percent in 1985, inflation rose to 40 percent in

September 1990, before declining to below 20 percent by May 1991. Swings in other price indices (wholesale prices, GDP deflator) were less pronounced; in particular, the wholesale price index showed a rather steady downward trend over the period 1983–90.

Furthermore, there is a clear seasonal component in the evolution of Ghana's consumer price index: prices tend to go up in the first half of the year, decrease during the summer months, and increase again during the last quarter of the year. This is mainly due to strong seasonality in food prices. However, non food prices show a similar but less pronounced seasonal pattern, which suggests a link between price developments in both categories, either directly through pricing policies for nonfood items that are related to changes in food prices or, indirectly, through cost factors such as the prices of petroleum products that exert a similar influence on food and nonfood prices.

Factors Determining Inflation

Food Supply

As indicated in Box 5, food prices have a large weight in the overall consumer price index. Since only a minor fraction of the food consumed in Ghana is imported, food prices are strongly influenced by developments in domestic food output, which has shown large swings during the 1980s owing mainly to variations in weather conditions

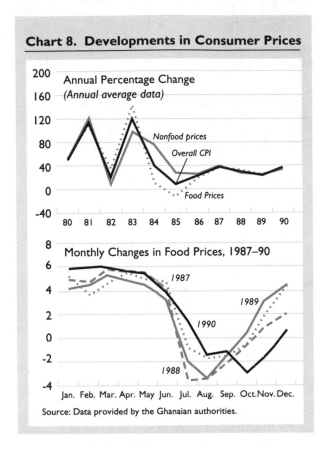

Chart 8. Developments in Consumer Prices

Source: Data provided by the Ghanaian authorities.

1987, fell to around 25 percent in 1989, and rose again to 37 percent in 1990 (Chart 8 and Table 14). On a twelve-month basis, inflation showed even larger movements: it fell to 23 percent by June 1989, accelerated to a peak of 41 percent by

Table 14. Price Developments, 1983–91
(Annual percentage changes)

| | Consumer Prices | | Wholesale Prices | GDP |
	End of period	Period average	Period average	Deflator
1983	142.4	122.8	128.9	123.1
1984	6.0	39.6	81.5	35.3
1985	19.5	10.4	56.3	20.7
1986	33.3	24.6	63.5	41.7
1987	34.2	39.8	41.4	39.2
1988	26.6	31.4	34.7	33.4
1989	30.5	25.2	25.5	28.3
1990	35.9	37.2	28.0[1]	30.0[1]
1991 January–May	19.8	24.6	...	...

Sources: Statistical Service; and IMF staff estimates.
[1] Estimate.

Box 5. Consumer Price Indices

Consumer prices in Ghana are measured on a monthly basis by the Statistical Service. Four consumer price indices are compiled: an urban index, a rural index, an index for Accra, and a national index. All four indices are Laspeyres-type index numbers that are derived as weighted averages of sub-indices for different categories of consumer goods, with 1977 as the base year. The composition of these indices differs, but in all four baskets food is by far the most important category, with shares of almost 50 percent, as indicated in Table 15.

In recent years, inflation in Accra has been higher than the national average, while inflation in rural areas has been lower. The differences were small, however, and in this study the rate of inflation will refer to changes in the national consumer price index.

Table 15. Composition of Consumer Price Indices
(In percent)

Index	Food	Clothing	Rent, Fuel & Power	Beverages & Tobacco	Household Equipment & Furniture	Transport & Communication	Miscellaneous
Urban	48.6	16.4	9.6	5.5	4.8	5.4	9.7
Rural	49.8	22.2	4.0	6.9	5.3	3.2	8.6
Accra	48.3	13.7	11.2	5.6	4.8	6.7	9.7
National	49.2	19.2	6.8	6.2	5.1	4.3	9.2

Source: Statistical Service.

(Table 16).[39] The severe drought of 1982–83 lowered agricultural output and caused a steep acceleration in food prices and the overall price level in 1983. The subsequent strong recovery in agricultural output led to a marked decline in food prices in the course of 1984 and a reduction in overall inflation to 6 percent by the end of that year. Agricultural output declined marginally during 1985–87, largely on account of insufficient rainfall, and the associated increase in food prices contributed to the resumption of an upward trend in the inflation rate. The return to normal weather conditions in 1988 and most of 1989 boosted agricultural output, resulting in a slowdown in inflation.

In late 1989 and the first half of 1990 food prices started to increase sharply. Two interrelated factors contributed to this development. First, flooding in some parts of the country in late 1989 disrupted the distribution of food supply, while late and insufficient rainfall during 1990 resulted in an estimated stagnation of agricultural output.[40]

Second, lower food supply and rising prices during the first half of 1990 appeared to have induced farmers and traders to build up stocks, partly for speculative purposes, which further reduced supply on the market during that period. Apart from these supply factors, the increase in retail petroleum prices during the first half of 1990 (by about 45 percent) exacerbated the upward pressure on food prices, given the importance of transportation costs in the price structure of domestic food output.[41]

In late 1990, however, food prices recorded sizable decreases, resulting from increased supply after late rains and, probably, sales from previously built-up stocks by farmers and traders. As illustrated in Chart 8, the pattern of food prices in 1990 was significantly different from the typical seasonal pattern; while in previous years food prices declined during July–September and increased during the last quarter of the year, in 1990 food prices started to decline in August and continued to decrease until December. In fact, the late rains have led to a temporary shift in the regular seasonal pattern in food output and food prices by about two months. This has led to a similar shift in the evolution of the overall consumer price index,

---

[39]For a theoretical analysis of the relationship between food supply and inflation in developing countries, see Edel (1969); for an empirical study, see Argy (1970).

[40]Rainfall is the predominant climatic factor for agricultural output in Ghana. The main agricultural regions have a bimodal rainfall pattern, with maximum rains in May/June and a second minor peak in September/October. Associated with the raining periods are two growing seasons: the major season which normally runs from March/April through July and the minor season from September through November/December.

[41]According to estimates by the Ministry of Agriculture, transportation costs account for about 50 percent of food prices; processing, distribution, and marketing costs for 20 percent; and farmers' income for 30 percent.

Table 16. Agricultural Output, Food Prices, and Inflation, 1983–91
(Annual percentage changes)

	Agricultural Output[1]	Food Prices[2]	National Consumer Price Index[2]
1983	−8.0	144.8	122.8
1984	15.4	12.0	39.6
1985	−1.7	−11.9	10.4
1986	0.2	20.3	24.6
1987	−0.3	38.5	39.8
1988	6.0	34.1	31.4
1989	5.2	25.1	25.2
1990	0.0[3]	40.2	37.2
1991 January–May	...	17.7	24.6

Sources: Statistical Service; and IMF staff estimates.
[1] Excluding cocoa, fishing, and forestry.
[2] Average data.
[3] Provisional estimate.

thus resulting in sharp increases in the rate of inflation during the third quarter of 1990 and a reversal of this movement during the last quarter of the year. In the first half of 1991, the increase in food prices was far less pronounced than in previous years, mainly as a result of the availability of large quantities of food from the delayed minor crop; the index for food prices in Accra in June 1991 was even lower than in June 1990.

The relationship between food output and food prices has been tested econometrically on the basis of quarterly data over the period beginning in the fourth quarter of 1984 and ending in the third quarter of 1990 (Appendix II). It appears that there is a significant relationship between changes in food prices and per capita growth in food output: a 1 percent increase in per capita output is estimated to lead to a reduction in food prices of 5–6 percent. In addition, fuel prices appear to be an important determinant as well: changes in fuel prices in the current and in the previous quarter both have a significant (and approximately equal) impact on the price index for food. Their combined long-term elasticity of 0.44 indicates that a 10 percent increase in fuel prices results in a 4–5 percent increase in food prices, which is well in accordance with the share of transport costs in the price buildup of food items.

Exchange Rate

Exchange rate developments can contribute to consumer price inflation either directly through their impact on the costs of imported consumer goods or indirectly through their impact on the costs of intermediate goods. In addition, exchange rate developments influence inflationary expectations, especially since the exchange rate is one of the most readily available indicators of price developments in Ghana. Over the past eight years, however, developments in domestic prices do not appear to have been closely correlated with developments in the official exchange rate. The very large changes that took place in the official exchange rate in the period 1983–87—the official cedi/U.S. dollar rate was raised from 2.8 cedis per U.S. dollar in early 1983 to an average of 154 cedis per U.S. dollar in 1987 (Table 17)—do not seem to have had a strong impact on recorded price developments. This holds true not only for the overall consumer price index, but also for the prices of tradables: while the official exchange rate of the cedi vis-à-vis the U.S. dollar (expressed as the domestic currency value of the unit of foreign currency) depreciated by a factor of 17 between 1983 and 1987, the prices of tradable goods in the consumer price index rose by a factor of 4 during the same period; at the same time the parallel market exchange rate depreciated by a factor of almost 3. These developments suggest that the prices of tradables reflected primarily the prevailing parallel market exchange rate rather than the official rate.

Even after the introduction of an auction system in 1986, many imported goods, particularly luxury consumer goods, continued to be financed by foreign exchange obtained in the parallel market. While access to the auction was gradually widened, it was not until January 1988 that almost all imports became eligible for funding at the auction. It is likely, however, that importers who had obtained foreign exchange at the more appreciated

Table 17. Exchange Rate Developments and Prices, 1983–91
(Period averages)

	Inflation		Official Cedi/U.S. Dollar Rate	Parallel Market Cedi/U.S. Dollar Rate	Spread Between Parallel Market/ Official Rate (In percent)	Nominal Effective Exchange Rate (1980=100)
	Tradable goods[1]	Nontradable goods[1]				
1983	109.0	133.5	8.8	76.7	2,088.6	54.8
1984	74.7	17.9	36.0	96.7	173.9	13.5
1985	26.9	− 3.6	54.4	131.3	142.7	9.9
1986	28.6	20.1	89.2	185.0	87.1	4.9
1987	42.2	37.0	153.7	224.1	35.8	2.9
1988	30.4	32.6	202.3	276.6	34.9	2.5
1989	24.9	25.6	270.0	345.6	27.5	2.2
1990	35.5	39.3	326.3	344.7	5.4	1.9
1991[2]	27.3	39.3	358.8	369.5	3.0	1.8

Sources: Statistical Service; data provided by the Ghanaian authorities; and IMF staff estimates.
[1]Components of the national consumer price index; annual percentage changes.
[2]Latest available figures; inflation data refer to the period up to May 1991, and exchange rate data to the first half of 1991.

official exchange rate have tried—as long as market conditions permitted such behavior—to set their prices in line with the higher parallel market rate rather than pass on their lower import costs to the consumer. This may have prolonged the relevance of the parallel market rate for the level of consumer prices. The economic importance of such behavior, however, diminished with the sharp narrowing of the spread between the parallel market rate and the official exchange rate after 1987 and its practical disappearance after the unification of the foreign exchange markets in April 1990.

The gradually declining influence of the parallel market rate on import prices and the corresponding increases in the importance of the official exchange rate make it difficult to quantify in a systematic way the impact of exchange rate developments on consumer prices. Simply comparing developments in the indices for tradables and nontradables, one could broadly argue that during the years 1983–87 there may have been upward pressure on the consumer price index from abroad, while since 1988 inflation seems to have been driven more by domestic rather than by foreign factors. In Appendix II an explicit assumption has been made about the relative impact of both the parallel market and the official exchange rate for movements in prices. It appears that a moving average of both rates, based on a gradually increasing relevance of the official rate, has had a significant effect on the price level during 1984–90.

Wages

Average monthly earnings per employee in Ghana increased sharply between 1983 and 1988.[42] Both in the private and public sectors real earnings quadrupled, exceeding by far any reasonable estimate of productivity growth during that period. The associated strong increase in unit labor costs in the private sector could have only in part been cushioned by a reduction in profit margins, thus exacerbating cost-push pressures. The large real increases in civil service wages most likely had a more indirect impact on inflationary pressures, serving as a yardstick in negotiations on private sector wages. The similar evolution of wages in the private and the public sectors during 1975–87 suggests a strong linkage between the two, although it does not indicate the direction of the causation. In addition, developments in public sector wages may have exerted a major influence on inflationary expectations.

These considerations would suggest a significant contribution of wage developments in inflation. However, the importance of this contribution would depend on the relative size of the formal employment sector in total economic activity and, more specifically, on the share in the consumer price index of goods produced in the formal employment sector. Although such data are not available, the small proportion of unionized labor in the total labor force would imply that the relative size of the formal employment sector is modest, while a large share of the basket used for compiling the consumer price index consists of goods

---

[42]However, the increase in real earnings during 1983–88 followed a sharp downward trend in the second half of the 1970s and the early 1980s; in fact, the levels reached in 1988 were still less than 50 percent of those in the mid-1970s.

(e.g., most food items) that are produced in the informal sector. Also, the sharp decline in real earnings that took place in the late 1970s and the early 1980s coincided with high inflation rates, indicating that developments in wages in the formal sector probably had only a limited effect on price developments during that period.

Until 1989, the salary level for the lowest grade in the civil service had been interpreted by the private sector as an unofficial indication of the minimum wage. In this respect, pay increases in the civil service tended to be treated as the floor for wage increases in the private sector. Together with average real earnings per employee, the level of this informal minimum wage had declined sharply in real terms in the period prior to 1983, but has since recovered somewhat. With a view to limiting the influence of pay developments in the civil service on wage changes in the private sector, the Government formally introduced with effect from January 1, 1989, a minimum wage and set its level at 170 cedis per day, a level lower than the equivalent salary for the lowest grade in the civil service and 16 percent higher than the unofficial minimum wage in 1988. Following the announcement of the new minimum wage, a large number of public entities and private enterprises adjusted their salary structures, resulting in a median wage increase of the order of 17 percent, before bargaining for the 1989 wage increase commenced. With a view to moderating wage claims and achieving a lower rate of inflation, the Government outlined in the 1989 budget the general principles that should guide increases in remuneration both in the public and the private sector, namely productivity gains in individual sectors, the expected rate of inflation, and the employers' ability to pay. While recent comprehensive data on private sector wage developments are not available, the wage increases agreed upon under collective bargaining agreements have been rather modest, with the principle of ability to pay reported to be gaining increasing importance. In 1989 and 1990, as well as in the budget for 1991, public sector wages were increased roughly in line with projected inflation, which in 1989 and 1990 was considerably lower than the actual outcome for inflation.[43] In March 1990 the daily minimum wage was raised by 28 percent to 218 cedis, reflecting the authorities' efforts to safeguard a minimum standard of living

for the unskilled part of the labor force. In general, it can be concluded that neither wages in the public sector nor wages in the official private sector are likely to have been a driving force behind inflationary pressures in Ghana in recent years.

Petroleum Prices

The retail prices of petroleum products, which are controlled by the authorities, were raised sharply during the first 18 months after the introduction of the economic recovery program: the price of premium gasoline was increased by 184 percent in 1983 and 143 percent in 1984 (Table 18).[44] In 1985 only two relatively moderate adjustments were made. Since then, changes in the retail prices of petroleum products have tended to be announced during the first quarter of the year, thereby accentuating the seasonal pattern of price developments. During 1986–89, the retail price of premium gasoline was raised at the beginning of each year by about 10 cedis a liter, resulting in declining changes in percentage terms from 43 percent in 1986 to 17 percent in 1989, which contributed to a slowdown in inflation during that period.

At the beginning of 1990 fuel prices were raised twice, by a cumulative total of about 45 percent, reflecting substantial increases in excise duties on petroleum products and higher costs. In September 1990, petroleum prices were raised further by more than 50 percent, mainly related to the sharp increase in world crude oil prices in August of that year. Finally, a fourth adjustment was made in early November 1990, when the retail price of premium gasoline was raised by 67 percent, bringing the total cumulative increase in 1990 to 266 percent, almost a quadrupling of the retail price within a year. This last increase in November was based on a full pass-through of the higher import costs; a further increase in excise duties from an average of 32 cedis per liter to an average of 65 cedis a liter for the main petroleum products;[45] the need to strengthen the financial position of the Ghana National Petroleum Corporation; and the need to bring retail prices more in line with those

---

[43]In early November 1990 the Government decided to accompany the increase in retail petroleum prices with a once-off wage and transportation allowance to civil servants for the last two months of the year, equivalent to 45 percent of basic pay per month.

[44]Premium gasoline is the main petroleum product sold in Ghana, with a market share of over 40 percent. Other important petroleum products are diesel, with a market share of about 34 percent and kerosene with a share in consumption of about 16 percent. Retail prices for the main petroleum products are adjusted simultaneously and generally by the same magnitude in percentage terms.

[45]This brought excise duties to the equivalent of about 35 percent of retail prices, compared with less than 10 percent at the beginning of 1990.

Table 18. Adjustments in the Retail Price of Gasoline, 1983–91

Date of Price Adjustment		Price of Premium Gasoline (In cedis per liter)	Percentage Change
1983	April 22	5.5	103.0
	October 11	7.7	40.0
1984	September 13	13.2	71.4
	October 5	18.7	41.7
1985	April 19	20.9	11.8
	September 9	23.1	10.5
1986	January 16	33.0	42.9
	March 20	30.8	− 6.7
	June 30	33.0	7.1
1987	February 1	41.8	26.6
1988	January 16	51.7	23.9
1989	January 13	60.6	17.0
1990	January 11	79.3	30.9
	March 31	88.1	11.1
	September 2	133.0	51.0
	November 2	222.0	66.9
1991	March 29	200.0	− 9.9

Source: Data provided by the Ghanaian authorities.

in neighboring countries.[46] In late March 1991 retail petroleum prices were lowered on average by about 12 percent, following the substantial decline in the crude oil prices during the preceding months. This decision reflected a shift by the Government towards a more flexible pricing mechanism for petroleum products, whereby changes in import costs will more readily be passed on to consumers, while protecting the tax elements in the price build-up.

The impact of fuel price changes on inflation can be traced through three channels: first, the direct impact through the weight of petroleum products in the consumer price index; second, indirectly via the prices of a broader spectrum of goods and services whose costs are influenced by fuel prices, mainly through transportation costs; and third, by the impact of fuel price changes on inflationary expectations. Given the limited availability of information on general price developments, fuel price changes in Ghana serve as an indicator of trends in the price level and thus clearly influence inflationary expectations. As a result of this last impact, changes in the retail price of petroleum products tend to trigger in-

creases in the prices of other products, even in the absence of a straightforward relationship.

The size of the direct impact can be gauged from the share of fuel items in the basket used for the consumer price index, which amounts to about 8 percent.[47] Estimates of the direct contribution of fuel price changes to inflation during 1983–90 are shown in Table 19. Excluding the direct impact of petroleum price increases on the price index in 1990 would reduce the end-of-period inflation rate from 36 percent to about 19 percent, a rate considerably lower than the corresponding "corrected" inflation in previous years. The overall impact of changes in petroleum prices on inflation is estimated empirically in Appendix II and appears to be about three times as high as the direct impact. This supports the hypothesis that fuel price changes have a significant impact on inflationary expectations and accordingly on pricing policies of products other than those directly influenced by petroleum costs.

Financial Policies and Domestic Demand

Large fiscal deficits in the early 1980s contributed to the liquidity overhang and inflation during

---

[46]Prior to 1990, petroleum prices in Ghana were among the lowest in sub-Saharan Africa, resulting in substantial smuggling across the borders. Since the last increase, the differences with neighboring countries have narrowed, although the price level of petroleum products in Ghana is still below the average for West African countries, excluding Nigeria.

[47]About 3.8 percentage points of the share of the category "rent, fuel, and power" and 4.2 percentage points of the share of the category "transport and communication" are directly related to fuel costs.

Table 19. Petroleum Price Increases and Inflation, 1983–90
(Annual percentage changes; end-of-period data)

	Consumer Prices	Retail Price of Premium Gasoline	Estimated Direct Impact of Petroleum Price Changes on Inflation	Change in Consumer Prices Excluding the Estimated Direct Impact of Petroleum Price Changes
1983	142.4	184.1	14.7	127.7
1984	6.0	142.9	11.4	−5.4
1985	19.5	23.5	1.9	17.6
1986	33.3	42.9	3.4	29.9
1987	34.2	26.6	2.1	32.1
1988	26.6	23.9	1.9	24.7
1989	30.5	17.0	1.4	29.1
1990	35.9	266.3	17.3	18.6

Sources: Data provided by the Ghanaian authorities; and IMF staff estimates.

those years.[48] However, the fiscal position has improved since 1983, with the narrow budgetary balance shifting into surplus (see Section V). Combined with large net inflows of concessional foreign assistance, this has facilitated sizable net repayments by the Government to the banking system since 1987. The potential inflationary impact of fiscal policy depends not only on developments in the budget deficit, but also on changes in indirect tax rates. In this regard, the sales tax rates and the excise duties on products other than petroleum have been raised only modestly since 1983. In addition, import duty rates were lowered in 1983, with a further small reduction in 1988. Furthermore, while the administered prices for electricity and transportation tariffs and water charges have been raised significantly, they appear to have followed rather than led inflationary developments during 1983–90.

Thus, it appears unlikely that fiscal developments formed a significant cause of inflationary pressure during the period under consideration. On the other hand, monetary policy has been more than accommodating until mid-1989, thereby contributing to demand-pull factors behind the inflationary process. As discussed above, in 1989 and 1990 inflationary pressures seem to have been accommodated to a significant extent by the excess liquidity built up in previous years, resulting in an

increasing velocity of circulation.[49] Measures to mop up excess liquidity, both in the banking system and in the economy, that were introduced toward the end of 1990, have contributed to a reduction in demand-pull inflation in late 1990 and early 1991.

Conclusions

Monetary policies since 1983 have been broadly successful in restraining the growth in domestic credit, while accommodating a strong expansion in real output and supporting the exchange rate policy. In addition, progress was made in shifting away from administrative controls toward an indirect system of monetary policy, with an increased reliance on market-based instruments of monetary control. At the same time, the restructuring of the banking system and the improved availability of financial instruments have enhanced the financial intermediation process and the incentives for financial savings. For most of the period, however, monetary policy has been less successful in bringing inflation down to a low level and restoring positive real interest rates; bank deposit and lending rates became positive in real terms essentially by mid-1991.

Inflation in Ghana appears to be determined to a substantial extent by developments in agricultural production. An abundant supply of foodstuffs leads to downward pressures on food prices and,

---

[48]In the absence of a well-developed capital market, domestic financing of fiscal deficits in developing countries generally takes place through bank credit, thereby contributing to monetary expansion (Aghevli and Khan (1977)). Subsequently, inflation induced by this monetary expansion may lead to a further worsening of the fiscal position, in which case a vicious circle can develop.

[49]An indication of the buildup of excess liquidity is the significant, but relatively low coefficient for increases in money supply in the estimated equation for inflation (see Appendix II).

given the high share of food items in the consumer price index, to a lower inflation rate. Bad crops, on the other hand, inevitably result in higher food prices and inflationary pressures. The exceptionally strong sensitivity of food prices to changes in domestic food production points to the importance of measures to improve the efficiency of marketing, storage, and distribution of food products with a view to increasing the returns to farmers, reducing the costs to consumers, and stimulating a more balanced supply.

This, of course, does not imply that inflation in Ghana is completely determined by structural factors and beyond the control of the authorities: inflationary processes have to be financed and their outcome depends strongly on the degree of monetary accommodation. Over the period 1983–89, money growth in Ghana has persistently been higher than the rate of increase in prices, owing largely to a higher-than-expected growth in the net foreign assets of the banking system. This has facilitated an accommodation of the inflationary pressures arising from developments in supply side and cost-push factors. A partial accommodation of the price effects of exogenous supply shocks is perhaps understandable, as a complete nonaccommodation of these effects through a very restrictive credit policy might not have been possible without a sharp decline in domestic demand and output. However, a more effective sterilization of the monetary impact of foreign inflows would have brought inflation further down during 1988–89

when agricultural output rose markedly, and would have reduced excess liquidity in the economy.

Inflationary pressures became stronger in late 1989 and most of 1990, mainly as a result of unfavorable weather conditions. In addition to these supply factors, sharp increases in the retail price of petroleum products, both in early 1990 and, due to developments in the Middle East, later in the year, added a cost-push element to the already existing inflationary pressures. Moreover, in the absence of regular information on general price developments, fuel price changes together with developments in the exchange rate and, to a lesser extent, wage developments serve as indicators of inflation. Therefore, these increases in domestic petroleum prices triggered a more general increase in prices.

In response, the authorities took restrictive monetary measures, the effects of which, however, were delayed by the prevailing excess liquidity in the economy. On the basis of empirical estimates of the main factors determining inflation, it is nevertheless clear that stepped-up efforts to absorb excess liquidity from the economy through the sale of Bank of Ghana instruments and sizable net repayments by the Government, resulting in a deceleration in the growth of broad money and a substantial increase in interest rates, have contributed to a moderation of the impact of the supply and cost-push factors on Ghana's inflation in the course of 1990, and have strongly supported the sharp decline in inflation in the first half of 1991.

VII Concluding Remarks

Ghana's economic performance has improved markedly since 1983, and the record of adjustment and growth during this period compares favorably with the experience of other developing countries. The improvement that has taken place in Ghana's economic situation appears to have been the result of three interrelated factors. First, the efforts undertaken to liberalize the economy, shifting from a centralized system with pervasive government controls to a market-determined environment, have been extensive and broad based. Second, effective implementation of the financial policies and structural reforms has been made possible by a strong political commitment to the adjustment process, supported by a domestic consensus on the need for economic reform. This commitment has been demonstrated on several occasions when a major strengthening of the adjustment strategy had become necessary to cope with the impact of exogenous shocks on Ghana's economy. Third, increasing external financial assistance and technical support from multilateral institutions and bilateral donors has facilitated the adjustment process. This assistance has been sustained at relatively high levels as donors appreciated Ghana's willingness to undertake far-reaching reforms and noted that external aid was not being wasted; in turn, sizable external financing has cushioned the impact on the economy of the steep decline in the terms of trade since 1986 and reinforced the Government's commitment to the reform process.

Ghana's adjustment experience since 1983 can be classified into three broad phases. During the first phase, spanning the period 1983–86, the emphasis of policies was on "getting the prices right," reducing the severe imbalances in government finances, and restraining credit expansion. Hence, the policy package included large discrete devaluations of the exchange rate, the lifting of domestic price controls, sizable increases in real producer prices for agricultural export crops, mobilization of government revenue through a broadening of the tax base and a strengthening of tax administration, and tightened control over government expenditure.

With the successful handling of the most immediate adjustment needs of the economy, the scope of reforms was broadened under the second phase, covering the period 1987–89, to include the initiation of structural changes which began to address the deep-rooted causes of imbalances in the economy and rebuild the productive base. During this phase, policy actions were focused on a comprehensive liberalization of the exchange and trade system, the divestiture program for the state enterprise sector, civil service reform to reduce the size of the civil service and increase remuneration levels, tax reform and improved tax administration, institutional and financial reforms to strengthen the domestic banking system, and substantial increases in government investment outlays for the rehabilitation of the economic and social infrastructure.

During 1990–91, Ghana's adjustment program entered into a third, perhaps more demanding, phase under which the implementation of structural and institutional reforms was accelerated, so as to achieve a more even balance between macroeconomic adjustment and structural policies; moreover, decisive steps were taken towards a market-oriented economy by the completion of exchange reform, increased reliance on market-based instruments of monetary policy, and significant improvements in the fiscal incentives for savings and investment by the private sector. At the same time, monetary management was reinforced and intensified efforts were made to reduce the inflation rate to a low and stable level. Clearly, continued heavy reliance on macroeconomic policies for attaining external viability and sustaining an adequate growth in output would have relatively high marginal costs in the absence of intensified and broad-based structural reforms. It had also become clear that a stronger increase was needed in private savings and investment in order to ensure a durable strengthening of the external position, boost the growth in employment and output, and sustain public support for the adjustment policies. In this context, further progress in the implementation of structural and institutional reforms, particularly in the areas of state enterprises and the domestic banking system, was essential for stimulating a stronger response by the private sector to the improved macroeconomic environment.

The design and sequencing of reforms since 1983 reflected a delicate balance between, on the one hand, the need to strengthen the complementarity of policy actions and thus contain the costs of adjustment and, on the other hand, the need not to overload the country's limited public and private managerial resources. Overall, while the sequencing of reforms was broadly appropriate, with the benefit of hindsight it is apparent that the economy would have benefited from a more forceful, and perhaps less gradual, implementation of the state enterprise and financial sector reforms as well as the liberalization of the institutional and administrative framework. This would have speeded up the development of private sector activity, including higher rates of savings and investment, as a consequence of the strengthening of the financial position of state enterprises and a deepening of the financial intermediation process resulting from a more efficient banking system. Admittedly, progress in these specific areas has been hampered partly by the limited availability of domestic technical skills and by the complexities inherent to the process of divestiture of state enterprises and of bank restructuring. The increasing demands generated by the policy and institutional reforms already implemented, or under preparation, have unavoidably strained the public sector's management and implementation capacity.

A key objective of the overall strategy during the past few years has been to ensure that a minimum critical mass of financial and structural reforms was in place, in part to adequately confront the severe imbalances in the economy and also to spread the benefits and costs of adjustment as evenly as possible over all segments of the society. Thus, for example, the policy of exchange rate depreciation has aided the process of fiscal adjustment, which in turn has allowed substantial increases in producer prices for cocoa, and boosted exports while simultaneously permitting sizable government investment in infrastructure. Similarly, the effectiveness of monetary policy reforms has been enhanced by the large repayments by the Government to the banking system and the improvements in the financial state of the domestic banking system.

Overall, Ghana has made significant progress in establishing the underlying conditions for a sustained expansion in output and employment in the years ahead and in smoothing the path of long-term economic development. However, as this is a protracted process that depends critically on the maintenance of confidence in the direction of policies, the adjustment efforts would need to be sustained for several years to come; in particular, policies will need to focus even more closely on the removal of the remaining structural, institutional, and financial impediments to growth, combined with the constant challenge of maintaining stable macroeconomic conditions.

Appendix I Structure of the Financial System

The banking system in Ghana comprises the Central Bank (Bank of Ghana), three large commercial banks (the Ghana Commercial Bank, the Standard Chartered Bank of Ghana, and the Barclays Bank of Ghana), seven so-called secondary banks (the Social Security Bank, the Bank of Housing and Construction, the National Savings and Credit Bank, the Agricultural Development Bank, the National Investment Bank, the Merchant Bank, and the Bank for Credit and Commerce), two new merchant banks that opened in 1990 (Ecobank Ghana and Continental Acceptances), a small cooperative bank, and over 100 small rural banks.

The Government fully owns or has a majority ownership in one of the primary banks and in all secondary banks except the Bank for Credit and Commerce, either directly or through the Bank of Ghana, the Social Security and National Investment Trust (SSNIT), and the State Insurance Company. The two new merchant banks established in 1990 are privately owned. Together with the existing Merchant Bank they specialize in corporate finance, advisory services, and money and capital market activities (underwriting, stock broking, mergers, and acquisitions). Three of the secondary banks are essentially development banks (the Agricultural Development Bank, the National Investment Bank, and the Bank for Housing and Construction), although the share of commercial banking activities in their overall operations has risen markedly under the new banking law, which entered into force in August 1989. The rural banks are essentially unit banks owned and managed by their respective local communities, established to mobilize resources in rural areas and extend credit locally; despite their large number, they account for only about 5 percent of the banking system's total assets and about 3 percent of total deposits.

With a view to enhancing the development of the domestic money market, a Consolidated Discount House was set up in November 1987, owned by a consortium of domestic banks and insurance companies. The Consolidated Discount House accepts short-term deposits from financial institutions and is required to hold at least 70 percent of its assets in short-term paper, while its borrowing is required not to exceed 25 times its capital and reserves. In June 1991 a second discount house (Securities Discount House), which was set up with the assistance of the International Finance Corporation, started its operations.

The nonbank financial sector, which is not regulated by the banking law, consists inter alia of about 20 insurance companies, the SSNIT, and a stock exchange. The SSNIT is a government-owned institution charged with collecting social security contributions and making social security payments upon retirement to participating workers. In 1991 a new pension scheme was introduced. In contrast to the past when workers received a lump-sum payment upon retirement, under the new scheme regular pension payments will be made, based on the average of the best three years salary as well as the duration of the contributions. The total contribution rate amounts to 17.5 percent and is applied to the sum of the basic salary and allowances (which in Ghana are of roughly equal importance). SSNIT receives contributions from both employers (12.5 percent) and employees (5 percent). All enterprises with five or more employees are required to become members of SSNIT. Until late 1986, SSNIT was required to invest its funds in government stock especially created for it, yielding about 6 percent, but it has since then been allowed to make its own choices regarding the composition of its assets. As a result, SSNIT has become a major purchaser of treasury bills and long-dated government stock, while recently it has shifted a substantial part of its portfolio into high-yielding short-term bills, as well as investments in real estate.

In November 1990, a stock exchange started its operations. Initial trading volumes were substantial, owing to the newly created opportunity for individual shareholders to divest and the prevailing interest among institutional investors to invest in stocks. Since then, however, trading volumes have been small, while only 11 companies have been listed so far. One of the factors behind this development has been the sharp increase in interest rates on short- and medium-term paper issued by the Government and the Bank of Ghana, which has reduced demand for stocks traded on the exchange. Trading volumes may pick up with the further realization of the Government's divestiture and privatization initiatives. In addition to the stock exchange, two other nonbank financial institutions were established in 1990: the Home Finance Company, which specializes in real estate financing, and the Export Finance Company, which provides mainly trade-related short-term loans to exporters.

Little information is available about the relative importance of transactions in the informal money market, comprising numerous credit unions, savings and loan institutions, and the so-called susumarket, which entails collection and redistribution of financial savings among groups of individuals. These informal markets were stimulated in the early 1980s by strongly negative real deposit rates, as well as a seriously eroded public confidence in the banking system. The recent decrease in the amount of currency in circulation and the relative increase in bank deposits suggests, however, that confidence in the formal banking system is gradually coming back.

As in the case of the rest of the economy, the financial position of the banking system in Ghana was adversely affected by the marked decline in economic activity in the period prior to 1983 and the associated sharp worsening in the profitability and overall financial wealth of the bulk of bank customers, particularly state enterprises. The financial difficulties of the banking system have unavoidably been exacerbated since 1983 by the impact of the sizable adjustments in the official external value of the cedi, which has affected the banks either directly (by raising their external liabilities) or indirectly (by weakening the financial position of some of their customers and in turn the quality of bank assets).

These problems were further aggravated by the weak bank supervision and regulatory framework, which did not enforce uniform and appropriate accounting standards, particularly with regard to the treatment of interest income on nonperforming loans and loan provisions, or set limits on bank exposure to single or related borrowers and on minimum bank capital adequacy ratios. Furthermore, the banks themselves have been characterized by inadequate management information and interbank control systems, as well as high operating costs.

In 1988, a comprehensive financial sector reform program was introduced, supported by the World Bank Group through a Financial Sector Adjustment Credit. The main objectives of this program were to (1) enhance the soundness of banking institutions by improving the regulatory framework and strengthening bank supervision by the central bank; (2) restructure financially distressed banks following the formulation of specific restructuring plans; and (3) improve resource mobilization and increase the efficiency of credit allocation by the banking system.

As a first step, an amended banking law was prepared, and enacted on August 8, 1989. This new act provided a sound prudential and regulatory base for Ghana's banking system by requiring banks to maintain a minimum capital base equivalent to 6 percent of net assets adjusted for risk, by setting uniform accounting and auditing standards and by introducing limits on risk exposure to single borrowers and sectors. Also, reporting requirements were strengthened, thus enabling the Bank of Ghana to improve its ability to effectively regulate the banking sector.

At the same time, a financial restructuring plan for the banking sector was developed, and approved by the Government in July 1989. The essence of this restructuring plan was the removal from the banks' portfolio's of all the nonperforming loans and other claims on both state-owned enterprises and the private sector. In November 1989 the Bank of Ghana issued promissory notes to temporarily replace nonperforming loans or other government-guaranteed obligations to state-owned enterprises as of end-1988. After validation of these nonperforming assets, the promissory notes were either replaced by Bank of Ghana bonds, or offset against debts to the Bank of Ghana and the Government. Additional nonperforming claims on state-owned enterprises as of the end of 1989 were similarly replaced by Bank of Ghana bonds in December 1990. The bonds carry an interest rate of 12 percent and have maturities up to five years, including a two-year grace period.

A similar procedure took place with respect to the nonperforming claims on the private sector by the financially distressed banks. These nonperforming assets were replaced by Bank of Ghana promissory notes in June 1990, and after validation was completed at the end of 1990, were offset against debt or replaced by Bank of Ghana bonds. The bonds issued against nonperforming loans to the private sector carry an interest rate of 7, 8, or 9 percent depending on the quality of the replaced asset and have maturities of two to five years. In March 1991 the nonperforming private sector claims of the so-called sound banks were offset or replaced by Bank of Ghana bonds. In total, some 62 billion cedis (about US$170 million) of nonperforming assets, including off-balance-sheet items, have been replaced by Bank of Ghana bonds (totaling about 47 billion cedis) or offset against Bank of Ghana and government claims on the banks; the nonperforming loans amounted to 32 billion cedis, representing about 41 percent of total bank credit to the non-government sector outstanding at the end of 1989.

Mainly as a result of the offset or replacement of nonperforming assets, banks were able to meet the new capital adequacy requirements by the end of 1990. All of the more than 1,300 nonperforming bank assets have been passed on to a newly created and wholly government-owned agency, the Non-Performing Assets Recovery Trust (NPART), which will try to recover as much of these assets as possible. NPART is mandated to finish its operations by the end of 1995. The counterpart of the bonds issued by the Bank of Ghana against non-performing bank assets is formed by a blocked account containing the domestic currency value of foreign assistance related to the financial sector reform program.

In addition, individual restructuring plans for seven distressed banks have been formulated and started to be implemented, including proposals for solving the management, financial, and operational problems of these banks. Early in 1990, the Government changed the top management and reconstituted the boards of directors of all financially distressed banks, while some banks have established twinning arrangements with foreign financial institutions. The restructuring plans are aimed at a reduction in operating costs and increasing efficiency, inter alia by the adoption of new organizational structures, a reduction in staff, and the closing of unprofitable branches.

APPENDIX II   Empirical Estimates of Inflation

In order to assess the quantitative significance for inflation of the factors discussed in Section VI, a reduced form equation for inflation was estimated for the period 1984:Q4–1990:Q3. This equation was derived from a simplified structural model, which combines monetarist, cost-push, and structural elements in explaining inflation (Table 20).[50] In particular, it has been assumed that the economy comprises four kinds of goods: food, goods whose prices are controlled by the Government (petroleum products), other traded goods, and other nontraded goods. As Ghana is a price taker in world markets, a change in the price level of traded goods (PT) is determined by the change in the foreign price level (Pf) and the weighted average change in the official and the parallel market exchange rate (Eo and Ep, respectively):[51]

$$\mathring{P}T = \mathring{P}f + [b(t)\mathring{E}o + (1 - b(t))\mathring{E}p] \tag{1}$$

with $0 < b(t) < 1$ and $db(t)/dt > 0$

where $b(t)$ is the share of transactions funded at the official exchange rate, which is supposed to increase over time. The retail price of petroleum products (PET) is administratively set.

$$PET = \overline{PET} \tag{2}$$

Changes in food prices (PFD) are assumed to be a function of changes in domestic food supply per capita (SFD), petroleum prices (PET), and real income (y):

$$\mathring{P}FD = f(\mathring{S}FD, \mathring{P}ET, \mathring{y}) \tag{3}$$

Finally, the change in the price level of other nontradable goods (PNT) is assumed to be a function of excess demand (ED) in the goods market, changes in import prices, and the change in domestic unit costs (UDC):

$$\mathring{P}NT = f(ED, \mathring{P}f + [b(t)\mathring{E}o + (1 - b(t))\mathring{E}p], \mathring{U}DC) \tag{4}$$

Furthermore, it is assumed that excess demand for goods is reasonably approximated by the excess supply of money balances, which follows from Walras' Law, given the fact that the markets for other financial assets in Ghana are rudimentary. It is further postulated that actual money holdings adjust only gradually to their "desired" level as a result of high transaction costs in the money market. Desired money is assumed to be a function of real income, prices, bank deposit rates, and expected inflation.[52] The latter is assumed to be related to past inflation, changes in petroleum prices, and exchange rate developments.

The change in the general price level (P) is thus defined as the weighted average of changes in the prices of the four kinds of goods in the economy:

$$\mathring{P} = a_1\mathring{P}T + a_2\mathring{P}ET + a_3\mathring{P}FD$$
$$+ (1 - a_1 - a_2 - a_3)\mathring{P}NT \tag{5}$$

Variants of the reduced form equation for inflation derived from the simplified model described above were estimated, based on quarterly observations for the period beginning in the fourth quarter of 1984 and ending in the third quarter of 1990. Since there are no quarterly data available for per

---

[50]The basic structure has been derived from other work in this area (see for example Khan and Knight (1981), and Chhibber and Shafik (1990)), but differs in that explicit attention is given to the impact of agricultural bottlenecks and changes in the retail prices of petroleum products on inflation. For a similar study in which the structural factor of excess demand for agricultural production is combined with the monetarist factor of changes in the rate of growth of the money supply in order to explain changes in the general price level, see Argy (1970). Theoretical discussions of the relationship between the structuralist and the monetarist explanation of inflation are presented in Kirkpatrick and Nixson (1976), and London (1989).

[51]A dot over a variable indicates a percentage change from the previous period.

[52]No assumption was made with respect to the existence of money illusion, resulting in a nominal specification of the money demand function, and—after derivation of the reduced form—nominal money growth as the explanatory variable representing monetary expansion in the inflation function.

Table 20. Theoretical Model for Inflation

1. $\dot{P}T_t = \dot{P}f_t + [b_t\dot{E}o_t + (1-b_t)\dot{E}p_t]$; with $0 < b_t < 1$

2. $PET_t = \overline{PET}_t$

3. $\dot{P}FD_t = f(\dot{SFD}_t, \dot{PET}_t, \dot{y}_t)$

4. $\dot{P}NT_t = f(ED_t, \dot{P}f_t + [b_t\dot{E}o_t + (1-b_t)\dot{E}p_t], \dot{UDC}_t)$

5. $ED_t = f(Ms_t, Md_t)$

6. $Md_t = f(y_t, P_t, i_t, \dot{P}e_t)$

7. $\dot{P}e_t = f(\dot{P}_{t-1}, \dot{PET}_t, \dot{PET}_{t-1}, \dot{E}o_t, \dot{E}p_t)$

8. $\dot{P}_t = a_1\dot{P}T_t + a_2\dot{P}ET_t + a_3\dot{P}FD_t + (1-a_1-a_2-a_3)\dot{P}NT_t$;

    with $0 < a_1, a_2, a_3 < 1$

Notation:

PT	=	Prices of traded goods.
Pf	=	Import prices in foreign currency terms.
PET	=	Retail prices of petroleum products.
PFD	=	Food prices.
PNT	=	Prices of nontraded goods.
P	=	General price level.
$\dot{P}e$	=	Expected inflation.
Eo	=	Official exchange rate.
Ep	=	Parallel market exchange rate.
SFD	=	Domestic food supply per capita.
ED	=	Excess demand in the market for goods.
UDC	=	Unit domestic costs of nontraded goods.
y	=	Real GDP.
M	=	Broad money (M2).
i	=	Bank deposit rates.

capita food supply, a quarterly indicator was constructed, based on the annual national accounts estimate for real value added in agriculture (excluding cocoa, forestry, and fishing), population growth, and a simple seasonal pattern (based on information about the rain patterns) according to which food supply during the first half of the year is lower than the annual average, while supply during the rest of the year is above average.[53]

Given the volatility in quarterly changes in money supply and the relevance of underlying monetary developments for inflation, the average increase in broad money in the current and the two preceding quarters ($AM2$) was selected as the ex-

planatory variable representing money growth.[54] Limited data availability did not allow the explicit inclusion of quarterly variables for real income and changes in unit domestic costs, although changes in per capita food supply and petroleum prices could serve as rough approximations.[55] Interest rate coefficients appeared insignificant, which can be attributed to the lack of movement in interest rates during the period under consideration.

The econometric results of a regression of food prices and of several specifications of the reduced form inflation equation are summarized in Table 21. All the regressions were estimated using ordinary least squares with a first-order autoregressive correction.[56] The first regression indicates that food prices are strongly influenced by changes in domestic food supply per capita and by current and lagged changes in petroleum prices. Changes in these two variables are also key determinants of developments in consumer prices, though their quantitative importance is roughly half that for food prices; the coefficients of SFD and PET in equation (1) are about twice as large as in equations (2)–(5). Regressions (2) and (3) show that the nominal effective exchange rate is only significant when introduced together with foreign prices. However, these regressions exclude the effects on inflation of movements in the parallel market exchange rate. In order to incorporate these effects, the nominal effective exchange rate used in regression (4) was adjusted to reflect movements in the parallel market rate.[57] The coefficient of the change in import prices declines in comparison to regression (3) and becomes insignificant, providing some support to the view that the official exchange rate may have been more significant than the parallel market rate. As a compromise, regression (5) uses a crude measure of the weighted average nominal effective exchange rate ($NEER$-AV). In particular, it is assumed that the share of external transactions valued at the official exchange rate rose from 20 percent during

---

[53]Argy (1970) uses two alternative indices for excess demand for agricultural output: the first measure is the rate of growth of demand, based on an elasticity of demand with respect to population growth of one and an income elasticity of demand of 0.6, minus the actual growth of agricultural production, while the second measure is simply the average annual rate of change in food prices minus the average annual rate of change in the cost of living. The specification used in this paper is similar to Argy's first measure, the main difference being that no explicit income elasticity of demand is assumed. Argy's second measure is implicitly based on the assumption that nonfood prices are not affected by developments in food prices, which is unlikely in the case of Ghana.

---

[54]Average quarterly data for broad money were used, obtained from the IMF's *International Financial Statistics*.

[55]In addition, assuming that the trend level of income (permanent income) is more relevant for money demand than actual income, and that the trend growth in real income is rather stable over the period under consideration, excluding real income growth from the inflation function is largely reflected in a lower estimated value for the constant term in the estimated equation (see Vogel (1974), p.112).

[56]The use of an autoregressive correction mechanism gave better results than including lagged inflation as an explanatory variable.

[57]The revised nominal effective exchange rate ($NEER$-SP) is calculated as the original index multiplied by the ratio of the official cedi/U.S. dollar rate to the parallel market cedi/U.S. dollar rate.

Table 21. Summary of Econometric Results[1]

Regression	Endogenous Variable	Constant	$S\dot{F}D_t$	$\dot{A}M$	$P\dot{E}T_t$	$P\dot{E}T_{t-1}$	$\dot{P}f_t -$ NEÈR$-$SP$_t$	$\dot{P}f_t -$ NEÈR$-$AV$_t$	$\dot{P}f_t -$ NEÈR$_t$	NEÈR$_t$	$\bar{R}^2$	S.E.E.	F-test	D.W.	AR(1)
1	$P\dot{F}D$	2.025 (0.45)	−5.517 (8.17)		0.220 (3.56)	0.222 (4.69)					0.718	4.57	15.63	1.90	0.784 (6.48)
2	$\dot{P}$	0.234 (0.08)	−2.831 (6.18)	0.393 (1.92)	0.119 (2.84)	0.114 (3.62)				−0.099 (1.47)	0.766	2.57	13.58	1.72	0.763 (5.88)
3	$\dot{P}$	0.907 (0.33)	−2.543 (5.61)	0.323 (1.62)	0.102 (2.44)	0.102 (3.28)			0.125 (2.02)		0.787	2.45	15.17	1.76	0.765 (5.96)
4	$\dot{P}$	0.410 (0.16)	−2.605 (5.41)	0.407 (1.97)	0.141 (3.49)	0.110 (3.41)	0.048 (1.22)				0.761	2.59	13.23	1.63	0.708 (5.58)
5	$\dot{P}$	0.391 (0.15)	−2.609 (5.82)	0.394 (2.02)	0.132 (3.47)	0.112 (3.71)		0.084 (1.97)			0.787	2.45	15.15	1.66	0.741 (6.05)

[1]Estimated using Ordinary Least Squares with quarterly data for the period 1984:Q4–1990:Q3. T-statistics given in parentheses.

1983–85, to 60 percent during 1986–87, to 80 percent during 1988–89, and to 100 percent during the second and third quarters of 1990.

The regression results are satisfactory; they indicate a positive and significant coefficient (at a 90 percent probability level) for import prices, and properly signed and significant coefficients for all other variables. The predicted values for inflation appear to trace the actual seasonal developments reasonably well (Chart 9). The seasonal pattern is mainly explained by movements in agricultural supply; adding seasonal dummies to the equation resulted in insignificant coefficients both for food output and for most of the other explanatory variables. The elasticity of inflation with respect to current petroleum prices is about 0.13, which includes the direct effect through petroleum products represented in the consumer price index, estimated in Section VI at 0.08. The indirect effects are reflected in the coefficient of 0.11 for lagged petroleum prices. It should be noted that part of the impact of petroleum prices on inflation may reflect exchange rate developments, as retail price adjustments also covered changes in the cedi costs of U.S. dollar-denominated crude oil imports. This could explain, at least in part, the relatively low coefficient for the exchange rate of 0.08.

The coefficient for broad money of 0.39 is low as well,[58] which may however be related to the

---

[58]Greene (1989) estimated values between 0.55 (for current money growth) and 0.84 (for lagged money growth) in a study for African countries over the period 1977–88. London (1989) found a significant coefficient for money growth of 0.64 in an estimated inflation equation for Ghana for the period 1956–85, using dummies for the high inflation years 1981 and 1983. However, his study showed a very low (0.18) and insignificant estimate for the corresponding coefficient in a cross-section analysis for African countries for the subperiod 1980–

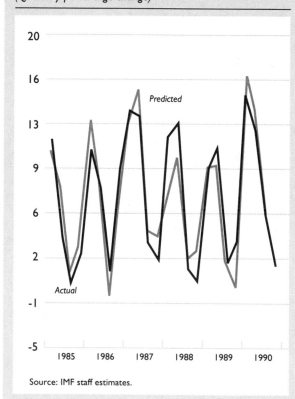

Chart 9. Actual and Predicted Inflation
(Quarterly percentage change)

Source: IMF staff estimates.

1985. Chhibber and Shafik found a short-run elasticity of inflation with respect to real money of about 0.4, while their long-run elasticity equaled 1. Amoako-Adu (1991) estimated a money demand function for Ghana for the period 1972–86 and found an income elasticity of 1.6, indicating a structural discrepancy between monetary and income developments that supports the low estimates for the coefficient for monetary expansion in inflation equations for Ghana.

buildup of excess liquidity during most of the period under consideration. In fact, broad money increased by a factor of seven during the period end-1984 until end-1990, while the price level increased by a factor of less than four during the same period. Overall, the results of the regression support the hypothesis that the large swings in inflation in Ghana in recent years have been strongly influenced by domestic supply shocks and domestic (petroleum price) and external (import prices) cost-push factors. The sharp reduction in the rate of monetary expansion since the beginning of 1990 was clearly reflected in the decrease in the rate of inflation in late 1990 and the first half of 1991, when the temporary effects on inflation of the sharp increases in petroleum prices and the delays in the availability of food output had worked out.

References

Addo, Joseph S., "Exchange Rate Reforms Under the Economic Recovery Program: Ghana's Experience," (unpublished; Washington: World Bank, 1990).

Amoako-Adu, Ben, "Demand for Money, Inflation, and Income Velocity: A Case Study of Ghana (1956–1986)," *Savings and Development*, Vol. 15, No. 1, 1991, pp. 53–66.

Aghevli, Bijan B., and Mohsin Kahn, "Inflationary Finance and the Dynamics of Inflation: Indonesia, 1952–72," *American Economic Review*, Vol. 67, 1977, pp. 390–403.

Aghevli, Bijan B., James M. Boughton, Peter J. Montiel, Delano Villanueva, and Geoffrey Woglom, *The Role of National Saving in the World Economy: Recent Trends and Prospects*, Occasional Paper 67 (Washington: International Monetary Fund, March 1990).

Argy, Victor, "Structural Inflation in Developing Countries," *Oxford Economic Papers*, Vol. 22, No. 1 (March 1970), pp. 73–85.

Arrau, Patricio, José de Gregorio, Carmen Reinhart, and Peter Wickham, "The Demand for Money in Developing Countries," IMF Working Paper No. 91/45 (Washington: International Monetary Fund, 1991).

Beaugrand, Philippe, "Ghana's Adjustment Program," *IMF Survey*, International Monetary Fund, Washington, November 1984, pp. 338–41.

Boateng, E. Oti, Kodwo Ewusi, Ravi Kanbur, and Andrew McKay, "A Poverty Profile for Ghana 1987–1988," SDA Working Paper 5 (Washington: World Bank, 1990).

Chand, Sheetal K., and Reinold H. van Til, "Ghana: Toward Successful Stabilization and Recovery," *Finance and Development*, International Monetary Fund and World Bank, Vol. 25 (March 1988), pp. 32–5.

Chhibber, Ajay, and Nemat Shafik, "Exchange Reform, Parallel Markets, and Inflation in Africa: The Case of Ghana," World Bank Working Paper WPS 427 (Washington: World Bank, May 1990).

Choudry, Nurun N., "Collection Lags, Fiscal Revenue and Inflationary Financing: Empirical Evidence and Analysis," IMF Working Paper 91/41 (Washington: International Monetary Fund, 1991).

Corden, W. Max, "Exchange Rate Policy in Developing Countries," World Bank Working Paper WPS 412 (Washington: World Bank, April 1990).

Edel, Matthew, *Food Supply and Inflation in Latin America* (Praeger, New York, 1969.)

Gilman, Martin G., "Heading for Currency Convertibility," *Finance and Development*, International Monetary Fund and World Bank, Vol. 27 (September 1990), pp. 32–4.

Greene, Joshua, "Inflation in African Countries: General Issues and Effects on the Financial Sector," IMF Working Paper 89/86 (Washington: International Monetary Fund, 1989).

Hadjimichael, Michael T., "Ghana: Lessons from the Experience with Inflation During 1983–88," (unpublished; Washington: International Monetary Fund, May 1989).

Heller, Peter S., A. Lans Bovenberg, Thanos Catsambas, Ke-Young Chu, and Parthasarathi Shome, *The Implications of Fund-Supported Adjustment Programs for Poverty: Experiences in Selected Countries*, Occasional Paper 58 (Washington: International Monetary Fund, May 1988).

International Monetary Fund, *International Financial Statistics* (Washington: International Monetary Fund, various issues.)

International Monetary Fund, *Interest Rate Policies in Developing Countries*, Occasional Paper 22 (Washington: International Monetary Fund, October 1983).

International Monetary Fund, *World Economic Outlook* (Washington: International Monetary Fund, May 1991.)

Khan, Mohsin, "Monetary Shocks and the Dynamics of Inflation," *Staff Papers*, International Monetary Fund, Vol. 27 (June 1980), pp. 250–84.

Khan, Mohsin, and Malcolm D. Knight, "Stabilization Programs in Developing Countries: A Formal Framework," *Staff Papers*, International Monetary Fund, Vol. 28 (March 1981), pp. 1–53.

Kimaro, Sadikiel N., "Floating Exchange Rates in Africa," IMF Working Paper 88/47 (Washington: International Monetary Fund, June 1988).

Kirkpatrick, C.H., and F.I. Nixson, "The Origins of Inflation in Less Developed Countries: A Selective Review," in *Inflation in Open Economies*, ed. by M. Parkin and G. Zis (Manchester: Manchester University Press, 1976), pp. 126–74.

Leite, Sérgio Pereira, and V. Sundararajan, "Issues in Interest Rate Management and Liberalization," *Staff Papers*, International Monetary Fund, Vol. 37 (December 1990), pp. 735–52.

London, Anselm, "Money, Inflation, and Adjustment Policy in Africa: Some Further Evidence," *African Development Review*, African Development Bank, Vol. 1 (June 1989), pp. 87–111.

Pinto, Bryan R., "Black Markets for Foreign Exchange, Real Exchange Rates, and Inflation: Overnight versus Gradual Reform in Sub-Saharan Africa," World Bank Working Paper WPS 84 (Washington: World Bank, September 1988a).

Pinto, Bryan R., "Black Market Premia, Exchange Rate Unification, and Inflation in Sub-Saharan Africa," World Bank Working Paper WPS 37 (Washington: World Bank, 1988b).

Quirk, Peter J., Benedicte Vibe Christensen, Kyung-Mo Huh, and Toshihiko Sasaki, *Floating Exchange Rates in Developing Countries: Experience with Auction and Interbank Markets*, Occasional Paper 53, (Washington: International Monetary Fund, May 1987).

Quirk, Peter J., "Issues of Openness and Flexibility for Foreign Exchange Systems," IMF Working Paper 89/3 (Washington: International Monetary Fund, January 1989).

Tanzi, Vito, "Inflation, Lags in Collection, and the Real Value of Tax Revenue," *Staff Papers*, International Monetary Fund, Vol. 25 (March 1977), pp. 154–67.

Villanueva, Delano, and Abbas Mirakhor, "Strategies for Financial Reforms," *Staff Papers*, International Monetary Fund, Vol. 37 (September 1990), pp. 509–36.

Vogel, Robert C., "The Dynamics of Inflation in Latin America, 1950–1969," *American Economic Review*, Vol. 64, No. 1, 1974, pp. 102–12.

Recent Occasional Papers of the International Monetary Fund

63. Issues and Developments in International Trade Policy, by Margaret Kelly, Naheed Kirmani, Miranda Xafa, Clemens Boonekamp, and Peter Winglee. 1988.

62. The Common Agricultural Policy of the European Community: Principles and Consequences, by Julius Rosenblatt, Thomas Mayer, Kasper Bartholdy, Dimitrios Demekas, Sanjeev Gupta, and Leslie Lipschitz. 1988.

61. Policy Coordination in the European Monetary System. Part I: The European Monetary System: A Balance Between Rules and Discretion, by Manuel Guitián. Part II: Monetary Coordination Within the European Monetary System: Is There a Rule? by Massimo Russo and Giuseppe Tullio. 1988.

60. Policies for Developing Forward Foreign Exchange Markets, by Peter J. Quirk, Graham Hacche, Viktor Schoofs, and Lothar Weniger. 1988.

59. Measurement of Fiscal Impact: Methodological Issues, edited by Mario I. Blejer and Ke-Young Chu. 1988.

58. The Implications of Fund-Supported Adjustment Programs for Poverty: Experiences in Selected Countries, by Peter S. Heller, A. Lans Bovenberg, Thanos Catsambas, Ke-Young Chu, and Parthasarathi Shome. 1988.

57. The Search for Efficiency in the Adjustment Process: Spain in the 1980s, by Augusto Lopez-Claros. 1988.

56. Privatization and Public Enterprises, by Richard Hemming and Ali M. Mansoor. 1988.

55. Theoretical Aspects of the Design of Fund-Supported Adjustment Programs: A Study by the Research Department of the International Monetary Fund. 1987.

54. Protection and Liberalization: A Review of Analytical Issues, by W. Max Corden. 1987.

53. Floating Exchange Rates in Developing Countries: Experience with Auction and Interbank Markets, by Peter J. Quirk, Benedicte Vibe Christensen, Kyung-Mo Huh, and Toshihiko Sasaki. 1987.

52. Structural Reform, Stabilization, and Growth in Turkey, by George Kopits. 1987.

51. The Role of the SDR in the International Monetary System: Studies by the Research and Treasurer's Departments of the International Monetary Fund. 1987.

50. Strengthening the International Monetary System: Exchange Rates, Surveillance, and Objective Indicators, by Andrew Crockett and Morris Goldstein. 1987.

49. Islamic Banking, by Zubair Iqbal and Abbas Mirakhor. 1987.

48. The European Monetary System: Recent Developments, by Horst Ungerer, Owen Evans, Thomas Mayer, and Philip Young. 1986.

47. Aging and Social Expenditure in the Major Industrial Countries, 1980–2025, by Peter S. Heller, Richard Hemming, Peter W. Kohnert, and a Staff Team from the Fiscal Affairs Department. 1986.

46. Fund-Supported Programs, Fiscal Policy, and Income Distribution: A Study by the Fiscal Affairs Department of the International Monetary Fund. 1986.

45. Switzerland's Role as an International Financial Center, by Benedicte Vibe Christensen. 1986.

44. A Review of the Fiscal Impulse Measure, by Peter S. Heller, Richard D. Haas, and Ahsan H. Mansur. 1986.

42. Global Effects of Fund-Supported Adjustment Programs, by Morris Goldstein. 1986.

41. Fund-Supported Adjustment Programs and Economic Growth, by Mohsin S. Kahn and Malcolm D. Knight. 1985.

39. A Case of Successful Adjustment: Korea's Experience During 1980–84, by Bijan B. Aghevli and Jorge Márquez-Ruarte. 1985.

Note: For information on the title and availability of Occasional Papers not listed, please consult the IMF *Publications Catalog* or contact IMF Publication Services. Occasional Paper Nos. 5–26 are $5.00 a copy (academic rate: $3.00); Nos. 27–64 are $7.50 a copy (academic rate: $4.50); and from No. 65 on, the price is $10.00 a copy (academic rate: $7.50).